His Grace
A Battle Won

His Grace
A Battle Won

A Missionary's Journey
from Tragedy to Triumph

Dana McCutchen

LIFE SENTENCE
Publishing, LLC

His Grace – A Battle Won | Dana McCutchen

All Scripture taken from the KJV

PRINTED IN THE UNITED STATES OF AMERICA

First edition published 2013

LIFE SENTENCE Publishing books are available at discounted prices for ministries and other outreach. Find out more by contacting info@lifesentencepubishing.com

LIFE SENTENCE Publishing and its logo are trademarks of

LIFE SENTENCE Publishing, LLC
P.O. BOX 652
Abbotsford, WI 54405

www.lifesentencepublishing.com

Like us on Facebook

ISBN: 978-1-62245-068-8

This book is available from lifesentencepublishing.com, amazon.com, Barnes & Noble, and your local Christian Bookstore

Cover Designer: Amber Burger

Editor: Mary Vesperman

Share this book on Facebook

Contents

PREFACE

From Tragedy to Triumph

My life story as a missionary wife and a mother of two, with unforeseen, life-changing experiences, which, through adversity, has made me a stronger Christian, helping me to see first-hand the magnificent power of God's awesome and sustaining grace.

My desire in writing this book is that it will touch the reader in such a way that he or she will come away with a greater love for our Lord and Savior.

Through each difficulty they face in life, they will be able to say, "Thank you, sweet Jesus."

"Pray without ceasing."

Prayerfully,
Dana McCutchen

CHAPTER ONE

STRANGE NOISES

Where was that sound coming from? It sounded like a subdued high-pitched screech. I tried to focus my attention on the message that Mark had prepared for the people that night as he had done so many times while on deputation in 1990, yet still, that bizarre sound forced me to look around to see what parent wasn't taking note of their unruly child.

I was shocked by what I discovered. How could it be that *I* was that parent? Our Shaunna, nine years old at the time, was sitting precariously in her own little world, unaware of any disturbance around her. I had to reach over Justin, our six-year-old, to get Shaunna's attention to behave and quit making those noises. She looked at me as if she had no idea what I was talking about.

Determination set in, for I was not going to have disobedient kids on deputation. Oh, if I only knew then what I know now! "Seasoned" veteran wives were quick to fill me in on all the do's and don'ts of how to raise your kids on deputation. I was green behind the ears. How was I to know that they did not have the perfect children? Perfect children — did they exist? I didn't think so, but apparently missionary children were expected to be well-mannered at <u>all</u> times, Bible scholars, completely adaptable to change, able to sit quietly through a two-hour service after riding in the car for fourteen hours, and a zillion other "perfect" criteria that make for a perfect missionary kid.

Once again, I reached over and told Shaunna that if she didn't behave, I would have to take her out and give her a spanking for insisting on making those noises. She looked at me in a puzzled way and said, "Momma, what noises?" I just knew that the pastor had out his "little black book" of missionaries not to support, and our name would surely be on it.

Unfortunately, I was a basket case for the first six months of deputation. I heard all kinds of horror stories about how pastors based their support of a missionary family on the behavior of the kids. I was told that missionary kids should never speak unless spoken to, give the slightest hint of too much energy while in church, fall asleep while their dad was preaching, chew gum, talk loudly, cry when having to leave Mom and Dad to go to their own Sunday School classes, accidentally wet the bed when staying in people's homes, voice that they didn't like spinach, and so on.

How was I to control Shaunna's outbursts? What forms of discipline should I use? How severe should I be? How in the world would we ever survive two years of deputation? I tried to be gentle yet firm in disciplining Shaunna, but what broke my heart were the tears streaming down her sweet young face as she cried, "Momma, what noises? What did I do wrong?" My eyes filled with tears as I saw the bewildered look on her face. I wondered what was wrong with our Shaunna. By God's grace, we made it through our first six months of deputation, *alive*.

As soon as we pulled into our hometown, Arlington, Texas, we made an appointment for Shaunna to see a pediatric neurologist. A tall, lanky doctor in his mid-30's came to greet us in the waiting room at Cook Children's Hospital. He was a nice enough man, and he led us into a cheery, bright colorful room filled with puzzles, games and toys. Shaunna immediately found a toy and planted herself on the carpeted floor. As we talked, the doctor uttered the words Tourette's Syndrome. I could feel my world falling apart. I just knew that our Shaunna was going to die from some terrible disease. He explained that Tourette's Syndrome is a neurological disorder that produces involuntary movements and sounds, known as "tics." What we didn't know was that OCD (Obsessive Compulsive Disorder), ADD (Attention Deficit Disorder), ADHD (Attention Deficit Hyperactivity Disorder), and Anxiety and Panic Disorder can accompany this syndrome known as Tourette's.

The doctor assured us that she would not die, which is true, but we were misinformed in many ways about this disorder that affects millions of children and adults throughout the world. The doctor said that she would grow out of it – **she won't.** He feels medicines don't help – **they do.** In his opinion, psychologists aren't much help – **they are.** Well, at least we had a diagnosis. The doctor made us aware that Tourette's is not a habit; therefore, it should not be punished. The guilt I felt from the months of reprimanding Shaunna was just too overwhelming. I remember crying in the doctor's office, thinking what a terrible mom I must be. Mark and I gathered Shaunna in our arms and thanked the doctor for his time.

I now had a new strategy, but would the churches be receptive to this bizarre disorder called Tourette's? Remember those "seasoned" veteran wives? My heart ached for them as I thought about all the blessings they missed because they listened to the "seasoned" veteran wives of their time. The pastors and members were full of compassion as Mark and I explained this new milestone in our lives known as Tourette's, and no, pastors do not carry around a little black book ready to strike a missionary off their list. We found the pastors to be a great source of comfort and full of wisdom, as well as offering a sense of humor. That's a good thing when you're traveling with small children. You never know what they're going to say.

Remember the saying, *Out of the mouth of babes?* We had just finished services in Oklahoma and were on our way to eat lunch with the pastor and his wife. The pastor invited us to ride with them in their car, recommending that Justin sit in the front with them. He explained that this would leave room for Mark, Shaunna and me to sit in the back seat. Everything was fine until I heard the pastor ask Justin what he liked to eat. I held my breath, hoping that the pastor had a good sense of humor, knowing that little five-year-old boys have an imagination all their own. Justin looked up at the pastor and said, "I like to eat telephone poles, frogs, and dirt." *Okay,* I thought. *That's it. There goes our support.* In all his seriousness, the pastor looked down at Justin while driving to the restaurant and responded, "Son, eating telephone poles here in Oklahoma is against the law." Justin laughed mischievously, and I breathed a sigh of relief.

———

Do you ever wonder if your kids are *really* listening to the message? I will answer that question with this story. Mark preached a message using the text from Matthew chapter five. Just as he was about to instruct the congregation to turn to the book of Matthew, Justin, still five years old, turned to the people behind us and said, "My dad's going to tell you to turn to Matthew chapter five." I wanted to die of embarrassment. They probably figured that Matthew chapter five was Mark's only message.

———

On one of our many trips to the north, we pulled into Johnstown, New York, a beautiful town away from all the hustle and bustle of the city life. Our host family took such great care of us. We were about to head for services, when I reminded Justin, now six years old, to brush his teeth. He made his way up the narrow stairs to do as he had been instructed. Not two minutes later, he hurried down the wooden stairs holding his mouth, stating that it was burning. I asked him to show me the tube of toothpaste. I read the lettering. No wonder his mouth was burning – he used BENGAY˙ muscle cream, mistaking it for toothpaste!

———————

While in Washington, D.C., we took the kids to see the White House and other historical places. While standing in line to take a tour of the White House, Shaunna politely asked one of the guards standing close by if he had seen *"Bro Bush"* that day. We all got a kick out of that one. The guard even managed a crooked smile.

I will praise thee; for I am fearfully and wonderfully made: marvelous are thy works: and that my soul knoweth right well (Psalm 139:14).

CHAPTER TWO

FAITH ISSUES

*H*ave you ever been to Steamboat Springs, Colorado? For most of the year, this gorgeous tourist town gets oodles of snow. During the month of July, the residents happily shed their heavy coats, snow boots, and woolen mittens, and throw on an array of tank tops, running shorts, and flip-flops. Mark was at the wheel (keen on getting to Colorado by day's end), listening to some southern gospel music. I was engrossed in a novel, and the kids – what were the kids doing? I turned slightly to find Shaunna busy with her artwork, but what about Justin? I half expected to find him asleep, but apparently he had become bored and decided to play with one of Mark's tennis shoes, dangling it by the shoestring – *out the window*. What possesses kids to do such things? I told him to put the shoe on the floorboard while I found him something to play with. I rummaged through my purse and found one of his toy cars. I said, "Justin, look what I found." When he didn't answer, I turned around to find him nodding off to sleep.

After a long, tiresome trip, we all barreled out of the car and stretched our muscles. The church was located on a beautiful ranch. What a charming and relaxing area. I was relishing the thought of sleeping in the same bed for a solid week without having to lug our suitcases around, when my thoughts were interrupted by Mark's words, "Dana, have you seen my other tennis shoe?" I cringed as I thought,

Oh, Lord, please don't let it be that Justin dropped Mark's shoe on the freeway. When I heard Justin sobbing quietly, I instinctively knew the mystery of Mark's tennis shoe. Mark couldn't very well get around in his cowboy boots, so we had a mission to accomplish.

After checking out the shoe stores in town, we quickly surmised that a $150.00 pair of tennis shoes was definitely out of our budget. The townspeople directed us to an antique store nearby but informed us that most likely it just contained antique furniture. I thought to myself, *Well, you're probably right, but you know, God **is** the God of the impossible.* We easily found the antique store and proceeded to enter. I had instructed Shaunna and Justin not to touch anything. *Ralph Wimm, a missionary to Mexico who went to be with the Lord some years ago, used to tell Shaunna and Justin to put their hands behind their backs as he took them on museum excursions.* There were lots of beautifully finished roll top desks and other various antique furniture items. We turned a corner and there – perched on an antique table – were a pair of men's almost-new, size 7 ½ *New Balance* tennis shoes. These were definitely in our budget – a modest $3.00 investment. *Thank you, God, for having a sense of humor and testing our faith,* I breathed.

Isn't it interesting how the Lord uses the faith of a child to teach us an important lesson? We, along with Ed and Cindy Richards, were in a conference together with Pastor Nitz in Titusville, Florida. After church services, Pastor Nitz took all of us out for lunch. Shaunna, Justin, and T.J. Richards were sitting in a booth next to the adults. At the end of our meal, Pastor Nitz reached into his pants pocket and pulled out three crisp five-dollar bills for Shaunna, Justin and T.J. Their faces brightened with surprise over this unexpected treat. We all thanked Pastor Nitz for the lunch, fellowship, and generous offering given to the kids, and went our separate ways.

About an hour down the road, raindrops started hitting the windshield. Shortly after, our right back tire went flat. Mark pulled off to the shoulder. I instructed Shaunna and Justin to stay in the car. By this time, it was raining steadily, even a downpour at times. Mark walked to the back of the car and opened the trunk. He had to remove all of our suitcases, the display, and schooling materials to get to the spare tire. I was holding an umbrella over Mark's head as he removed the spare tire and proceeded to change the flat one. I found a piece of cardboard to lay on the ground to protect Mark's pants from the wet ground. Finally, after about an hour, we were on the road again. Thankfully, we made it to the Sunday night services on time.

Mark and I prayed that the Lord would provide better tires for our car. The associate pastor was standing in for the pastor that evening. When it came time for the offering, Mark reached into his wallet and pulled out some dollar bills. I looked over at Shaunna as the offering basket was coming her way. She had her five dollars out. I quietly whispered to her that she didn't need to give her five dollars, because Dad had money for her to give. Figuring that she'd want to buy something special for herself, I expected her to tuck the five dollars back into her purse. Now, here I am, a grown woman trying to teach our children about the blessings of giving to God, but finding myself telling Shaunna to put her money away. She sure taught me a lesson. She whispered back that the Lord told her to give her five dollars to him. I nodded and smiled that the Lord would indeed bless her. After services, the associate pastor asked us to stand at the back of the church. Oh, an important detail is that this happened to be my birthday, October 6. Remember the five dollars that Shaunna gave to the Lord? The Lord taught us a lesson of giving through the faith and obedience of a child.

A dear lady in the church asked about my birth date. When I told her that it was that day, she started crying. She said that her husband had died the year before on October 6. She wanted to give me something. She held out a white envelope and asked me to take it. I thanked this sweet lady for her gift of love. Shortly after, the associate pastor felt burdened to buy new tires for our car. He had no clue of our flat tire on the way to the church. We were rejoicing over God's goodness but He wasn't through yet. On our way out the door, a couple handed Mark a white envelope and asked us to use the gift to help purchase a piece of property in Brazil. We thanked everyone and headed to the hotel.

Inside our room, we opened the envelopes from the dear lady and the sweet young couple. As I opened the white envelope from the lady, I noticed a $100 dollar note. I was overwhelmed by her generosity. I was so glad that I had jotted down her name. Mark opened the other white envelope and found a check written in the amount of $1000.00. God is so good! Shaunna and Justin got in on the excitement too. We all sat down together on one of the double beds and thanked God for His goodness and provision. We thanked Shaunna for her obedience to the Lord and asked forgiveness for our lack of belief. Through Shaunna's willingness to obey God and giving her surprise five dollars to the Lord, the Lord in turn blessed our family by giving us brand new tires for our car, money to help us purchase property in Brazil and extra money to help with our expenses. Shaunna was grinning from ear to ear, knowing that God had blessed us through her giving. Justin had been quiet through the whole ordeal. I could tell he was thinking. Maybe he wanted to do the same. Finally, he spoke. "Dad, do I have to give my five dollars too?" We all laughed, telling him only to give it if the Lord told him to so. He sure seemed satisfied with that answer!

———

Fayetteville, Arkansas. There is a really nice state park in the city known as "Devil's Den." I know, you are probably asking how it can be nice with a name like that. The four of us had just finished exploring the caves, and then decided to have some fun on the playground. There was a steep grassy incline making its way down to the swings and slides. Apparently, I was not surefooted, for I found myself on the ground, writhing in pain. Oh, the pain in my foot! Mark was trying to console me and trying to look at my ankle. The kids came running up the hill, finding me on the ground with Mark hovering over me. Through their screams, he was finally able to explain to them that I had fallen on the slippery grass on the way to the playground. Mark instructed Shaunna to sit behind me, so I could rest up against her. Shaunna said that I looked as white as a sheet, ready to pass out. Unfortunately, there were no other adults close by to help.

After leaving me in Shaunna's care, Mark ran to the first aid station. The station was closed. Mark noticed a sign taped to the front door. It read, *In case of an emergency, please drive to the nearest hospital.* Apparently, there had been other emergencies in the past. Our car was back at the campground, about five minutes away. Mark knew he would need to hurry. He wasn't sure if I had sustained other injuries in my fall. He ran the whole way through heavy brush, ravines, and potholes, careful not to injure himself along the way. He returned with the car, and he and Shaunna gently lifted and placed me in the front seat.

We arrived at the hospital safely. X-rays were taken which showed a split bone on the top of my foot. I was on crutches for the following six weeks. I sure had some challenges maneuvering the crutches up and down stairs of the many churches we visited after my mishap. Don't get me wrong now, for we sure had some laughs too, especially when I needed to elevate my wrapped foot on the dashboard. You see, after a while, my foot would start perspiring. The weather was extremely hot, which caused us to run the air conditioner quite a bit. The perspiration from my foot, along with the air conditioning, didn't make for the most ideal situation. Mark and the kids all adapted well to the smell permeating from my stinky foot.

By the third week on crutches, I was pretty much a pro. We were headed for Tennessee for a Sunday morning service. Between Sunday school and the church service, Mark and I noticed the pastor and the deacons smoking cigars on the back porch of the church. We thought that was kind of odd. That was a new one for me. The pastor's wife was leading the music and then stopped for prayer. All of a sudden, the men at the front of the church began praying in unison – very loudly. It startled me, for I wasn't used to being in that kind of service.

I remember seeing the church sign with the word Baptist on it. Oh, well, I guess this is the way they do things in this part of the country. Soon, Mark was tapping me on the shoulder. He quietly whispered to me, "Hey, the pastor's wife wants you to go up front." "Now?" I said. "Yes," Mark confirmed, "Now." "Why?" I asked. "They're still praying!" "Well," he responded, "You're either gonna sing or they're gonna heal you." I didn't know what to expect. But don't worry; they didn't try to heal me. The pastor's wife told me to sing, but I thought, *Sing now? The men are still praying – very loudly.* I voiced my thoughts to her and she said, "Yes, praise God, sing now!" It was really strange for me to be singing with all those men praying loudly at the same time.

I was so ready for deputation to end. Would it ever end? It would and it did in the fall of 1992.

But my God shall supply all your need according to his riches in glory by Christ Jesus (Philippians 4:19).

CHAPTER THREE

NEW BEGINNINGS

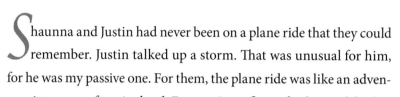

Shaunna and Justin had never been on a plane ride that they could remember. Justin talked up a storm. That was unusual for him, for he was my passive one. For them, the plane ride was like an adventure into a new frontier land. For me, I was flying farther and farther away from what was familiar and loved. I knew that God wanted us in Brazil, and I wanted to be in surrender to Him, but oh, how my heart ached to be back in my own hometown.

During the flight, people all around me were talking Portuguese and laughing at each other's stories. Every time I closed my eyes, I saw my mom and dad's country home. I could hear the melody of their wind chimes gently blowing in the wind. The picture of Dad on the riding mower with the sun beating down on his weathered neck was a beautiful sight. The smell of cut green grass made me feel so clean. Suddenly, my mind was jolted back to the reality of being in a foreign country as the jetliner landed at midnight on that balmy October night. The flight had little turbulence, but I was still so glad to be on solid ground. As we exited the plane, I could feel the dampness and the heaviness of the humidity in my lungs. Dim lights lit the airstrip that enabled us to see the shuttle bus nearby. As we followed everyone else, I was hoping this bus would take us to the airport. Picture this scenario. You and your husband arrive in a foreign country, you have two small sleepy children in tow, you don't speak the language, and you have eight footlockers to maneuver through customs. Justin, being only a 7-year-old, was very cranky, not only because of the time of night, but also because of the motion sickness pill I had given to him hours before, but had not taken effect until we landed. I guess that's par for the course. Somehow, we made it through immigration.

My uncle and aunt, Bill and Mary Horton, were waiting for us as we came through the customs check. I could barely make out Uncle Bill's head craning over the high wall that separated them from the inside of the airport. They were sure a welcome sight. They have been working as missionaries in northern Brazil for over thirty years. After a hoopla of hugs and kisses, my first inclination was to get back on that plane and head for home, but then it dawned on me, *this was my home; for however long God chose to use us here.*

Belém, Pará. This city is vastly populated, located at the mouth of the Amazon River. Lush rain forests surround this predominately Catholic city of approximately three million people. Located just sixty miles south of the equator, Brazil's temperature stays at a constant degree all year long. Because of the abundance of rain, vegetation is everywhere. The banana trees are truly amazing with their oversized leafs. Have you ever seen a chocolate tree? What impressed me most was the rubber tree. Yes, you read right, the rubber tree. Rubber is one of the main exports in Brazil. The Açai tree was Justin's favorite to climb. Açai resembles a cranberry in size with a hard red covering. As a mom, I have to tell you that I was scared to death as Justin shimmied up that 30-foot-high tree. Can you believe that he asked me if he could carry a machete in his mouth to cut down the Açai fruit? Of course, I said no. What mom wouldn't? Shaunna learned the art of descending a tree in a heartbeat after she saw a black bird with a long beak with multiple colors. We told her she had just been introduced to a Toucan. The look on her face was so hilarious.

After a couple of days in the country, we had to report to immigration for the processing of our carteiras (it's kind of like a green card), which would allow us to stay in the country. When the immigration people noted that Mark's passport said Mark McCutchen and his visa said Mark S. McCutchen, they ordered Mark back to the United States. Can you guess their reasoning? He was not the same person! I thought to myself, *If he's going, then we're all going!* It seems all a blur now, but I vaguely recall Uncle Bill trying to reason with a Portuguese lady who sat behind a scratched, dirty window, that Mark McCutchen was indeed Mark S. McCutchen. After what seemed to be hours but was only a few minutes, a tall, dark-skinned man emerged from a large office situated a few feet behind the main corridor. He overheard the conversation and quickly resolved the whole mix-up. I don't think that the lady was very happy that things were in order. She seemed to want to make the transition hard for us. I prayed a prayer of thanksgiving for the kind man who made it possible for us to stay in the country.

For the first three weeks, a nauseated feeling consumed my whole body. The smells of the market just about got the best of me. It was important for me to make the trips to the market, because this was the way I would be selecting the meats for my family. I think it would have been better if we had all been vegetarians! My first lesson was to learn how to choose my chickens for dinner. Now, I'm talking about live chickens! A boy of about ten years of age reached in and grabbed the squawking chicken that I had chosen from the coop, and the awful, disgusting process began. Some of you may be thinking, *but you're a Texas girl.* That's right, but I'm a *city* Texas girl!

The young boy cut a slit in the chicken's throat and then placed it upside down in a large vat. I watched the boy as he removed the chicken from the vat by its feet and then proceeded to another makeshift machine that I can only describe as a huge hot roller. He placed the chicken on the roller and flipped the switch. Suddenly, feathers were flying everywhere, and the dead chicken's head was bobbing up and down. After most of the feathers were removed, he lowered the dead chicken into a huge pot of boiling water to remove any remaining feathers. That was bad enough, but what was even worse was the fact that he bagged the chicken, feet and all, and placed the bag in my hands. The feeling of those dead, yet warm, chicken feet in the palm of my hand and the beady black eyes staring back at me just about made me sick to my stomach. I don't think I ate for at least an entire month!

Trips to the grocery store were forever a laughing matter. I just couldn't seem to get my words right for the right product. For instance, when I asked for condensed milk, I actually asked the patron for condemned milk. No wonder he looked at me in a strange way. I learned that batata fritas are French-fries instead of barata fritas which are fried cockroaches. Maybe those are a delicacy in some parts of the world, but I hope it's not in Brazil. Mamãos are papaya while mamães are mothers. One night at church, I told Mark to look at the mamães up in the tree. I thought I had used the correct pronunciation. Uncle Bill teased me, saying that mothers usually aren't found in a tree. The odors from the fish department aren't explainable. I think the odor was so bad because the fish are laid out to dry using salt to preserve them. I wasn't quite sure of the name for baking powder, but I had no problem finding the candy bar isle.

Every Monday night was set aside as family night. To celebrate, I'd buy four large candy bars, along with four large-size soft drinks. We all looked forward to our once-a-week family night. One of the rooms in our rented home was air-conditioned, so our books and papers would not mold or mildew. The room offered such comfort to us. We hung redes (hammocks) across the room, watched our favorite TV programs that had been taped from the States, and then bedded down for the night, swinging ourselves to sleep. Isn't it wonderful how the Lord gives us such precious memories?

For we are laborers together with God... (I Corinthians 3:9a)

CHAPTER FOUR

LEARNING HOW THINGS ARE DONE

I remember being in tears one day, because I couldn't seem to open the dishwashing detergent bottle. I tried everything in my power to get that plastic bottle open. At that time, Belém didn't have the pop-up tops to disperse the liquid. After an hour or so of trying to figure out the secret to opening the bottle, I gave up and went to my neighbor for help. I found the secret. Simply puncture the top with a toothpick. To the Brazilian, it was the most logical thing to do. I soon learned that toothpicks were not just for cleaning one's teeth.

Once settled into our house, Aunt Mary arranged for me to have a maid. Now, I know what you're thinking, *A maid?* It's not like you think. A maid is a lifesaver to those in the ministry. While Uncle Bill, Inácio and Nata were teaching Mark and me the Portuguese language, our maid was cooking and cleaning. I remember setting out the whole chicken in the refrigerator and gesturing to the maid that we would eat this for dinner. After language school, I walked into the kitchen of our spacious home and smelled the delicious aroma of chicken, steamed rice, and beans. It was so nice to have our dinner cooked. Learning a new language sure builds up an appetite. That night we sat down for dinner but soon realized that there were pieces of that chicken that I didn't recognize or even knew existed. I mentioned it to Uncle Bill the next day. He understood and instructed our maid not to include any of the intestines, head, eyes, or feet. Our maid took the unwanted pieces, along with the chicken head, to her dogs. We found out later that they are excellent nutrition for animals. When our maid was done for the day, she would try to tell me so, but I had no idea what she was saying. She started using gestures, which was kind of like playing charades. She would stand in front of me and imitate taking a shower. I didn't catch on at first, but then realized what she was trying to say when she pretended to be washing her hair.

After settling into our home, our next project was finding a car. Uncle Bill and Aunt Mary were always so gracious to pick us up for church or anywhere else we needed to go. Because our road was so bumpy, Uncle Bill suggested that we meet him out at the main road. By the time Mark and I made it to the highway, we were drenched in sweat. We had not yet grown accustomed to the excruciating heat. It was worse on Mark, for I was usually cold natured. After making it to the end of our road, we caught our breath and then piled into Uncle Bill's Volkswagen van, already loaded with some of the Brazilian church members. We greeted everyone with our limited vocabulary. I enjoyed trying to speak the language, even though it wasn't correct. I found out though, that I needed to be more careful with my pronunciation, because I unknowingly cussed everyone out in the van, trying to ask them how they were doing. Everyone looked at me in shock, but Aunt Mary cleared it all up in a hurry.

I was still adjusting to the severity of the roads. There were so many holes, and I don't mean just potholes! These holes were so big that I lost sight of the road ahead of us. I remember one such time when Mark and I were with Uncle Bill in the front seat, headed for the grocery store. The road dipped and water stood where the van would need to cross. I thought, *Now, how are we ever going to get through all that water?* As we waded our way through in the van, Uncle

Bill instructed us to lift our feet. We did and then understood why. Water started pouring into the van through a hole in the floorboard. I thought about all the parasites in that water and silently prayed that Mark and I wouldn't get any diseases from that murky water. Readers, most of your missionaries in the interior find themselves needing to buy a new vehicle each term. The vehicles are not able to withstand the road conditions through all the torrential rains.

We were anxious to purchase our own car. Uncle Bill and Aunt Mary were in the process of building their house, which didn't leave them much time to help us find a car, so Mark took it upon himself to search for one. We knew how to conjugate two verbs, so Mark ventured out, praying that he could buy a vehicle with his limited vocabulary. About six hours later, I heard a car pull into our driveway. Wondering who would be visiting me, I looked out the window and saw Mark getting out of a small car. I couldn't believe my eyes! It was a bright red VW Gol (kind of like a VW Rabbit). I was so proud of him. Mark told me how he managed to communicate using the two verbs and sign language to get his point across. It turned out to be the best car we've ever had. Now, God did that!

We had some wonderful days, but we sure had some hard ones too. I tried to be strong for the kids. I didn't want Shaunna and Justin to see me crying, so I secretly cried every day for the first three months. I tried to keep my mind off of home by concentrating on learning the language, participating in the Bible Club, and mastering the cooking skills to prepare the meals made from scratch. Every time Mark left the house to check the mail, I would wait by the front door of our home, hoping to get some news from *home*. I could spot the return address a mile away – a letter from my mom, Shirley Brown. I could already feel my throat constricting from the huge lump that threatened to cut off my air supply. Tears threatened to spill over my hot cheeks. In my heart I was crying, *Oh, Mom! I miss you so much. Will we ever see each other again?* I could smell my mother's delicate scent in the glorious daffodils and daisies that abounded from beneath the ground. I could sense her closeness around me. I could hear her beautiful voice in the colorful birds perched nearby. It was then that I realized that God had truly blessed me. My mother's spirit would always be with me.

It was nearing Christmas, and Mark and I knew that for our marriage to survive the stress of learning the Portuguese language, we needed to be with other students to see how our language skills were progressing. Therefore, we made plans to leave the day after Christmas and purchased our tickets for the forty-two-hour bus ride from Belém to São Paulo. Flying was out of the question, for it was extremely expensive to fly within the country. Before we moved, we spent our first Thanksgiving and Christmas with Uncle Bill, Aunt Mary, their daughter, Tanya, and Brazilian friends. Tanya was married the week of Thanksgiving to a Brazilian man named Eduardo. Since Uncle Bill would be performing the wedding, he asked Mark to ask the question, Who gives this bride away? Mark faithfully practiced the question until he felt like he had the pronunciation down pat. Now, remember that we had only been in the country for four weeks. The time came for Mark to ask the question, which he did, but Uncle Bill, after giving Tanya away to Eduardo, lost his senses and was standing at the back of the church, proud as a peacock. Mark didn't know what to say. How could he? He only knew three verbs at the time. Mark just stood there, praying that Uncle Bill would realize that he was supposed to be where Mark was standing. Kyron, our cousin, spoke into the microphone, snapping Uncle Bill back to his senses.

Christmas Day dawned humid and muggy, but oh, what a wonderful time to celebrate our Lord's birth. The aroma of chicken and dressing, pumpkin pie, banana nut bread, and other succulent foods filled the air in the spacious home of my aunt and uncle. Mark, along

with Uncle Bill and the Brazilians, were all enjoying a game of soccer and volleyball. I was in the house talking with Aunt Mary about
lunch preparations, when Shaunna emerged from outside, apologizing for interrupting but stating that there was an emergency. She
explained that a rock had come out of nowhere, hit our windshield
and shattered it. After much interrogation, Shaunna came forth and
ashamedly admitted to accidentally shooting a rock with her new
slingshot. Apparently it had ricocheted off some other object and
hit the windshield. I guess you could say it was our fault too. I never
even thought to bring Christmas presents with us to Brazil. When
we started shopping for presents, I realized that everything was in
Portuguese, so we put our heads together and came up with gifts
like Legos, building blocks, and yes, that's right, *slingshots.* Whatever
possessed us to buy those I'll never know.

Back at Uncle Bill's place, we wanted to make sure and get home
before dark, so we packed up the car, minus a windshield, said our
good-byes to family and friends, and made our way home. Imagine
being in 100-degree weather, with 80 percent humidity, and no windshield. While Mark drove, I positioned a notebook in front of my face
to dodge the bugs. I could hear them splattering against the hard
cover. As I glanced over, I saw Mark's head moving from side to side,
trying to keep his mouth closed so he wouldn't swallow any bugs. By
this time I was laughing so hard my stomach ached. We stopped for
a red light and Mark said, "Dana, see that guy walking towards us?"
I nodded an affirmative yes, and he said mischievously, "Watch." As
the man neared our car, Mark lunged his upper torso through the
gaping hole where our windshield used to be. I don't think I've ever
seen a dark-skinned man turn white as a sheet. We laughed so hard
at the expression on that man's face that we almost wet our pants.
He's probably still running!

CHAPTER FIVE

SÃO PAULO

Forty-two hours later, we found ourselves at the bus station in São Paulo. What a trip. I'm glad it was uneventful, except for the toilet paper or should I say, sandpaper, which was sold at the entrance to the restroom. The paper was sold square by square. I can't remember how much money I spent just on toilet paper. I knew from then on to take my own.

Delbert Canright met us at the airport and drove us to his home for a much-needed rest. After a few days, we knew that this was the place God wanted us to be. We rested up for a week and then made the forty-two hour bus ride back to Belém to gather all of our belongings. Shaunna and Justin stayed with Delbert and Alice. Once in Belém, we packed all of our belongings and then made the crazy trip back to São Paulo. Halfway there, Mark started coughing on the bus. His breathing was labored and his cheeks were flushed. I was really getting concerned about him. We finally made it back to the bus station in São Paulo. Pat Shebester invited us to stay with her while looking for a house to rent. Two weeks passed, and the Lord provided us with a two bedroom duplex. The duplex was located in a quiet neighborhood with minimal traffic. Mark's condition had worsened. I didn't know of any doctors that Mark could see for his labored breathing. I knew that the hospital was about forty-five minutes away, but I sure didn't know how to get there by car. I dialed Pat's number, praying that she would be home. After a brief description of Mark's condition, she quickly came over and took Mark to her primary care doctor while I stayed at home with the kids. About two hours later, Pat called to say that Mark was headed for the hospital; he had pneumonia. The doctor said that most likely it was caused by the change in weather going from Belém to São Paulo in such a short amount of time. I was so scared to be by myself, but I knew that I needed to be strong for Shaunna and Justin. I didn't want them to see the fear in my face. Delbert and Alice were so good to take care of me and the kids. They passed by our house every day, asking if we needed anything.

I wondered if any of the doctors and nurses at the hospital knew how to speak English. By now, Mark and I knew enough of the language to speak with four verbs. Mark called the next day to tell me how he had fared his first day in the hospital. According to him, the triage nurse didn't use any of those verbs, because he didn't know what she was saying, but he sure understood the long silver needle in her hand. Once in his private room, another nurse came in and said, "I speak English." Mark was beside himself. He was so relieved that someone could speak English. She left for a few minutes, only to return with yet another silver needle, repeating her phrase, "I speak English." Apparently, that was the extent of her English vocabulary. After a week on oxygen, Mark felt like new again.

Learning the Portuguese language was both frustrating and amusing at the same time. Our co-worker, Jerry Lantz, turned forty years old halfway through our language study. We needed candles. What's a birthday cake without candles? Mark approached Domingos, the deacon in the church, and asked if he could find forty candles for Pastor Jerry's cake. Well, the word he used *sounded* like candles, but that was definitely not the word he used. The word for candles is "velas," but he accidentally added a letter to this simple word. So, actually when he asked for candles, he used the word "velhas." In essence, he asked the deacon, "Do you have forty old women for Pastor Jerry's cake?" The deacon responded with, "Well, if he had forty old women, what would he do with them?" That story is still circulating among the Brazilians.

One crisp morning, I sent Justin to the vegetable market, located across the street from our duplex, to buy some (cenoras) carrots. He politely asked the lady for one kilo of senhoras (ladies). Her sense of humor put Justin at ease and playfully commented on his mistake of words. The Easter holiday was approaching, so Shaunna was memorizing a verse about the Passover for Sunday school. When time came for her to recite her verse, she proudly stood and recited it word for word. Her verse was Jesus is our Páscoa (Passover), but she inadvertently said, "Jesus is our Paçoca" (sweet peanut brittle). She was so cute, standing there so proud of herself. Well, Jesus is sweet! The congregation thoroughly enjoyed her mistake.

I remember the time at a church function when Mark ate what appeared to be a tuna fish sandwich. Well, it definitely wasn't tuna fish. He couldn't figure out what that awful taste was. He unknowingly mistook the sardines for tuna. Shaunna did the same thing, but when she found out that she had just eaten two sardine packed sandwiches, she just about lost all her dinner. She said that even though it didn't taste awful to her, she still couldn't imagine eating a fish that people used as bait.

In that first year of our language study, I was introduced to Atalias, who is now one of my dearest friends. She was always conscious of how I was feeling. One Saturday a month I would receive a call from my mom and dad, Jay and Shirley Brown. How well I remember the anticipation of that phone call. Because we didn't have our own home phone, I would use Delbert and Alice Canright's phone. They lived just down the street from us. (The Canrights are now retired missionaries living in Arlington, Texas.) I still remember the anticipation of waiting for the phone to ring. When I heard my parents' voices on the other end, I would just about cry the whole time. It was wonderful to catch up on what was going on. We were able to talk for about twenty minutes. The cost was so expensive, about $50.00. Atalias always knew when my mom and dad had called. She could feel the homesickness in my heart as the tears flowed down my cheeks. Her shoulder was always available for me to cry on. At first, we could only smile at each other. She knew no English, and I barely knew any Portuguese. She taught me so much. She has been single all these years, waiting for the right guy to come along. Well, her marital status changed as of August 17, 2002. She married our co-worker, Jerry Lantz. They are great servants of the Lord.

Mark and I attended language school with five other couples. The teachers come from various parts of Brazil. All students were allowed to teach their first lesson or preach their first sermon in their native tongue. After that, it was Portuguese all the way.

Halfway through our language study, Mark contracted the mumps. He was quarantined to the house for twenty-one days, which meant that I would have to take the bus ride alone. Sheer horror at the thought of taking the bus by myself made me shudder. On one particular day, I couldn't remember which stop to get off at on the way home. I calculated the ride had been about an hour or so, so I started watching for our neighborhood area, but the streets all looked familiar. I pulled the string for the driver to stop at the next stop. He did so, but then I soon realized I had made a mistake, so I motioned for him to keep going. I pulled the string repeatedly, realizing every time that it was not my stop.

One of the landmarks at our bus stop was a familiar looking *tree*, but that day all the trees looked the same. After about the seventh time of pulling the string, a young man nearby asked me if I was having a problem. I said to him, "I can't find my tree." I knew he thought I was wacko, but after explaining to him about the familiar tree, he asked me the name of my neighborhood. I told him, and he assured me that my stop, *along with my tree*, was coming up shortly. I thanked the Lord for the man's kindness. I thought I would be on that bus looking for my tree for the rest of my life!

While we studied the Portuguese language an hour and a half away from home, Shaunna and Justin attended the Pan American Christian Academy. They absolutely loved it. The teachers are well trained and love the ministry to which God has called them. Justin's first grade teacher, Miss Meacham, sure knew how to keep the kids' attention. In particular, Justin recalls how the class did math on the ceiling, using an overhead projector. Bob Brennan saw the potential that Shaunna had for playing soccer. He taught her so much. She played the goalie position for the varsity team during her eighth grade year. Mrs. Limpic, the elementary school principal, put her whole heart and soul into the school. She is such a vital part of the school. Coach Fast taught Justin how to swim. He was deathly afraid of going near a swimming pool, lake or ocean, but Coach Fast had ways of teaching them how to swim. He set it up in phases. Within three weeks, Justin was swimming and loving it.

I can't recall how many times Shaunna came home with notes from her teacher asking us to help her control her outbursts. Her teachers viewed her outbursts as bad behavior, but Mark and I knew better, we just didn't know how to help her. We knew of no one else with Tourette's, therefore we silently suffered the battle alone. It wasn't long after, that I received a book from my mom, entitled, *Tourette's*

Syndrome, A Parent's Guide. It was then that we realized that the doctor in the States had misinformed us that Shaunna would outgrow her Tourette's; but on the contrary, she would learn to live with it on a daily basis. Shaunna exhibited many of the obsessive-compulsive behaviors (known as OCD) that were mentioned in the book. From the reading material, we knew that Shaunna was also suffering from ADD (Attention Deficit Disorder). After reading and digesting every page, we made it available to the school. The teachers understood more about Shaunna's difficulty holding in her tics. Her tests were given to her orally and were not timed. Her homework was modified to meet her needs. She had special helps from the high school kids in all of her classes. Her teachers worked with her, helping her to learn at her own pace. They will receive great blessings one day because of their sacrifices made.

After our year of language school, a couple by the name of Celso and Claudette, showed us an area that desperately needed an Independent Baptist Church. The Lord burdened our hearts for the people of Vargem Grande, farmland hit by a meteorite many years ago. The land mass is in the shape of a huge crater. Vargem Grande, which sits on the outskirts of the city of São Paulo, is predominately Catholic, with a sixty-five percent unemployment rate. Mark, along with the young people from the church in Varginha, distributed flyers announcing a special program from the Calvary Baptist Church of Vargem Grande. Our first church service was held in a storefront building about one kilometer away from the neighborhood. I actually expected the people to come in droves, but that was not to be. We did however, have two visitors that morning, April 29, 1994. You're probably thinking, *That's good that you had at least two visitors.* Normally, I would agree, but our two visitors were a rooster and a dog!

Our second service opened a way into Vargem Grande. A dear man by the name of Jonas visited our church and invited us to use his home in Vargem Grande for however long we needed. We were praising the Lord. In Jonas and Elizabeth's small home, people heard the Gospel for the very first time. I started teaching the women some of the Bible stories. They couldn't believe that Jochebed put Moses in the water. When I told them that we would continue the story the following week, they begged me to finish the story. How refreshing it was to see those ladies hearing the story of Moses for the first time.

On one occasion, I was teaching the kids and young people about Jonah and the whale. I knew my Portuguese wasn't great, but the Lord was working in their lives. I could see it in their faces. After the story, I gave an invitation. Mistakenly, I asked them to bow their hairs instead of their heads. Everyone lost it. They were all laughing. I thought, *Oh, good Dana, you really blew it this time.* That's what I was thinking, but the Lord had other plans. In spite of my blunder, the Holy Spirit still worked in the service. Ten precious souls were saved that day.

Our co-worker, Jerry Lantz, was in the States for his furlough, so we were using his car on occasion to keep it in running condition. At that time, we made visits on Wednesday nights before services. It was a nice night, so we told Shaunna and Justin that they could stay with their friends while we made visits. We dropped them off by the church and then proceeded to the bottom of the hill to visit one of the girls in our Sunday school class who had missed a couple of Sundays. As we pulled in front of their house and stepped out of the car, we noticed about five or six Suburbans, filled with military police and guard dogs, park behind us. Before I knew it, a sawed off shotgun was pointed at my temple. Police surrounded our car. I asked Mark in a low voice what I should do. He said, "Don't move a muscle." We knew all too well that many times the police shoot first and ask questions later. They quickly surmised that we were not the escaped prisoners from the prison located a few miles away. We waited nervously as the policemen searched all the neighboring homes to find the escaped convicts. Fortunately, we made it to church on time. Even though it was a scary time, I never felt afraid for my life. I knew that the Lord was in control of the whole situation and that His will would be done in our lives.

Do you have Thanksgiving and Christmas traditions? We do, both in the United States and in Brazil. In Brazil, every year for Thanksgiving, we pack up the car and head for the beach, a two-hour drive from São Paulo. The great thing about having Thanksgiving at the beach is that the beach is scattered with just a few people, unlike the thronging crowds during December, January, and February. Because the seasons are opposite the United States, these months are their summer months. June through August are their winter months. We've been celebrating Thanksgiving at the beach, while in Brazil, since 1992. A dear couple in our language class had an apartment two blocks from the beach. They graciously offered this apartment to other missionaries for a fraction of the cost. In the early nineties, semi-trucks and cars used the same road to travel down the mountain to get to the beach city, Guarajá.

Once in Guarajá, we could feel the clean air in our lungs. There's no pollution in this small, yet growing town. We usually spent seven to ten days basking in the sun and enjoying a much-needed rest from the responsibilities of work. Mark and the kids enjoyed riding the waves, using a body board and a huge inner tube, while my delight was sitting on the beach with one of those huge beach umbrellas protecting me from the sun rays, listening to music while translating songs into Portuguese. Playing in the water and translating songs sure builds up an appetite. One of our favorite beach vendors is João Batista. He sells coconut and roasted corn. It was amazing to watch him chop off the top of the coconut with his machete and insert a straw to sip out the coconut water. I've never acquired the taste for coconut water, but the meat of the coconut is really tasty.

One of my favorite and funniest memories on the beach is about the *lady in white*. I saw her at the other end of the beach walking our way. She had on a beautiful full-length white buffeted dress with a white turban wrapped around the top of her head. As she neared us, I could hear her calling out the product she was selling. Three young men were walking behind her carrying a makeshift cooler. I quickly reached into my bag and retrieved our digital camera. I thought, *Oh, I'd better take a picture to show the ladies in the church.* By this time, Mark and the kids were back on the beach with me, sitting in the sand. They too noticed the lady in the white dress. I could faintly hear her calling, "Carajé." She was selling some sort of food product. I wasn't really interested in the food, just the uniqueness of her appearance.

I took my camera out of the bag and looked up to find her standing in front of me. She was posing for me. She stood there, waiting patiently for me to take a picture of her. I took a couple of pictures, and they continued on their way. We were laughing so hard that we almost fell out of our chairs. If that wasn't bad enough, every time she made her way back to our spot on the beach, she would stop and pose for me. She wouldn't leave until I took another picture of her. I shared my experience with the ladies in the church and they all laughed heartily, informing me that *she* indeed was a *he*, a transvestite from Bahia, a northeastern state in Brazil. Apparently, it's a common sight in that part of the country.

Happy is the man that findeth wisdom, and the man that getteth understanding (Proverbs 3:13).

CHAPTER SIX

UNEXPLAINED CHANGES

At the beginning of Shaunna's sixth grade year, I was concerned about the change in her behavior. Thumb sucking became a daily ritual as she would sit and rock back and forth for what seemed to be forever. Because many Brazilian children suck their thumb into pre-adolescence, I assumed that thumb sucking was a security blanket for her. I tried to be gentle and non-judgmental as I explained that thumb sucking was for very small children. There were times when she would curl up on the couch with a blanket close to her face. I could tell that she was trying to suck her thumb without anyone noticing.

She no longer desired to visit with her friend, Adriana, or spend the weekend with her family. Adriana and her sister, Kelley had been saved under our ministry. Their mother, Lucia, also a Christian, had been coming for some time to the services. Olsvaldo, the father, was a drunkard and very seldom made his appearance. Shaunna's excuse not to visit with Adriana was that she wanted to be at home with us.

Not long after, she came to me and nervously reported that she and Adriana had walked to the nearby bread store early one morning. Adriana went to use the pay phone located across the street from the bread store. Shaunna had been instructed to stay at the store and wait for Adriana's return. Shaunna recounted to me, in almost a whisper, how a drunkard approached her in the bread store. At that moment, my heart began beating rapidly. I was crying inside, not wanting to hear that my daughter had been hurt. When I asked Shaunna what the man had done, she replied, "Oh, nothing, he just put his hand over my mouth and knocked me down." My heart breathed a huge sigh of relief. I asked her if she was sure that nothing else had happened, and she assured me that nothing had.

Shaunna's social skills plummeted during the fall semester of her eighth grade. She was doing very poorly at interacting socially, especially with the other boys in her class. She stopped taking an interest in how she looked. Food seemed to occupy her every thought. She didn't care that the boys made fun of her and called her fat.

Mark and I were pleading with God that He would lead our paths in the right direction to be able to help Shaunna with her difficulties in social interaction. Shaunna had changed. It was hard to put our finger on it, but she wasn't the same Shaunna we knew. She was afraid of the dark, which was unusual for her. She seemed distant, not the carefree loving daughter that we had just a year earlier. It seemed like she was dying inside, but I had no clue as to why this change had come over her.

During our third year on the field, the Brazilian cruzeiro plummeted and forced most of the WBF (World Baptist Fellowship) missionary families home to raise more support. Our rent doubled overnight from $300.00 to $600.00, which caused us to prepare for our furlough in August 1995.

The culture shock of being back in the United States was probably hardest on Shaunna. She had just turned thirteen years old and didn't know the latest artists in teenage music or the trendy clothes that were in style. She was ten when we left for Brazil but was a teenager when we returned. She didn't have the opportunity to grow with the other teens. Most teens weren't interested in knowing about her adventures in Brazil or the lonely times of homesickness she experienced. I think my hardest challenge was to rid Shaunna and Justin of their head lice. That was so embarrassing. I remember at one point seeing the lice jumping from Shaunna's hair. It seemed I had tried every shampoo to rid her of the head lice that were determined to make her hair a nesting ground. A short haircut was the only answer. That did the trick. Many people believe that lice affect only those on low income or unsanitary people. Lice affect people of any race, color or income.

Justin traveled with us most of the time on our furlough, and Shaunna, because she was so prone to carsickness, opted to stay with my parents or friends in the church. I was amazed at all the new technology that had come about while we were in Brazil. One such technology that the kids loved, but I was not so inclined to jump on board with was the new style of music. Music had never been a battle with our kids but that was soon to change. Shaunna and Justin's leisure time in Brazil was flying kites, playing marbles and kicking the soccer ball around. Now, their focus was on music videos, teen magazines, and the latest style of clothes. I remember listening to James Dobson on the radio about what battles to pick with your kids. A caller mentioned that she had two children who wanted to listen to a secular music group. Her daughters were the same ages as Shaunna and Justin. James Dobson's response was for the parent to ask if what their kids are doing will matter in ten years. If so, then say no and set your foot down. If not, then control the situation with moderation. Mark and I decided to diligently try and apply that rule of thumb to every situation we came across with our kids. It's been a great guideline for us, and I encourage other parents to try this technique.

Our year on furlough had come to an end. Our bags were packed and last-minute details were checked and double-checked. I was so ready to sleep in my own bed and trade out our suitcases for dressers.

Three weeks before our departure, I woke up with a weird tingling sensation in my mouth. The left side of my tongue, along with the left side of my face, was numb. My left eye wouldn't close and my mouth was crooked, drooping to the left side. I hollered for Mark in the other room, telling him that I thought I was having a stroke. It was Saturday, and our doctor's office wasn't open, so we jumped in the car and sped down to the nearest emergency clinic. The doctor at the walk-in clinic reassured me that I wasn't having a stroke but was suffering from a case of Bell's palsy. Bell's palsy is a virus that settles in the 7th facial nerve, causing paralysis to one side of the face. Have you ever tried to eat cereal with a droopy mouth? Trust me when I say that it's a laughing matter. My friends and family would deliberately make me laugh, so they could see my smile curve up on one side while simultaneously droop on the other. It was all in good fun though, for I knew they were concerned about me.

Shaunna became extremely emotional when it came time to leave. I passed it off as what all missionary kids go through they hate to say good bye to their family and friends, only Shaunna was crying for a different reason, one of which I had no idea.

Put on the whole armor of God, that ye may be able to stand against the wiles of the devil (Ephesians 6:11).

CHAPTER SEVEN

TOURETTE'S AGAIN?

Back in Brazil, Shaunna made excuses as to why she couldn't go to church. She became very belligerent and moody. We assumed she was going through a rebellious stage at fourteen years of age. That year was very strenuous for all of us. We couldn't understand what had caused the change in her. Her thumb sucking had resumed. I felt helpless. What could I do to discourage what seemed to be "rebellion"? While trying to help Shaunna through her difficulties, we noticed in January of 1997 that Justin was manifesting some of the same tics that Shaunna was experiencing. I couldn't believe that *both* of our kids could have Tourette's.

It was at that particular time that I was introduced to Pat Hofheiser, via e-mail. Because her kids have Tourette's as well, we were able to swap stories and encourage each other. Thanks Pat!

We observed Justin through the beginning months of that year. We finally concluded that Justin indeed was suffering from Tourette's. To be sure, we made an appointment with an English speaking pediatric neurologist. He confirmed that Tourette's was the diagnosis. Justin was heartbroken. Every twelve-year old boy wants to be "normal." When he realized he had TS, his first question to the doctor was, "Will my children have Tourette's Syndrome?" The doctor replied that there would be a fifty percent chance for his children to inherit the disorder. We didn't understand why Justin's TS was manifesting itself at the age of twelve, because it usually manifests itself during the early elementary years, but God knew exactly what He was doing.

Justin's TS was much more severe than Shaunna's. His fifth grade teacher thought it wise to inform the other children in the classroom why Justin made the sounds he did or had a hard time when it came to teasing. She presented it very well to the children, hoping to shed some light on why Justin acted the way he did. I had forgotten how cruel kids can really be. While the teacher stepped out of the room, the other students passed around a white piece of paper with a picture of half of a brain. It still breaks my heart to think of what ridicule he endured during the fifth grade. Aggression was the hardest part of Justin's Tourette's. Many neurologists feel that aggression is a major part of TS. When Justin came out of a rage attack, he was always extremely remorseful over his actions. Mark and I, along with the school principal, set up a *safe* place on the school campus. When Justin felt like he couldn't control his rage, a teacher who knew of his attacks would meet him there to help him through his rage.

Anything could set off a rage attack – not being able to find his math book and being embarrassed because of it; relentless teasing by others on the soccer field; having to ask for directions to be repeated or not understanding what he read for the day's lesson. Most teachers understood, but there were some who just didn't know how to handle situations like those mentioned above. We knew that Justin needed counseling and possibly medication. At that time, Brazil wasn't qualified to treat TS. On counsel from our pastor, Dr. D.L. Moody, and our mission director, Tommy Raley, we decided the best route was to return to the States and seek medical help.

As I look back over my life, I'm so glad that our ways aren't God's ways. We didn't understand His ways in 1997 when He moved us from Brazil back to the United States. Shaunna, Justin and I made the ten-hour flight together to the States, while Mark stayed in Brazil to take care of some last-minute details concerning the church.

Trust in the Lord with all thine heart; and lean not unto thine own understanding (Proverbs 3:5).

CHAPTER EIGHT

SILENT SUFFERING

*I*was sitting in my mom and dad's study, thinking how nice it was to see everyone again, when a noise startled me. Shaunna was standing in the doorway and approached me once again about the day at the bread store.

"Mom," she said.

"Yes, honey, what is it?" I replied.

Her lower lip started to quiver. She was trying to control the tears that threatened to spill onto her cheeks. Then she told me.

"Uh, I was, uh, raped in Brazil."

What? I couldn't believe what I was hearing.

My insides cried out, *No! Please God, No!* I felt numb all over. I was trying to find my voice to comfort my daughter. I held her and we both cried. She so sweetly said, "It's okay, Momma. Those things happen." I thought to myself, *Yes, tragically they do happen, but how could God let this happen to my precious daughter?* I couldn't believe what I was hearing. So many emotions were going through me.

There's a process to grief and everyone goes through it. Mark and I went through denial, anger, sadness, loneliness and so many more emotions that I can't remember. The key to victory in overcoming the grief process is when we can come through it – praising God, not blaming Him.

She went back to the day of the attack. It was a cold morning, around 6:00 o'clock. She was instructed by her friend, Adriana, to wait at the bread store while she made a quick call on the pay phone located just across the street. The bread store was busy with mothers buying bread while attending to their children. Several men were at the bar getting drunk, and others not far behind. Suddenly, a man grabbed her from behind, covered her mouth, and dragged her to the back of the building. She recalls hitting, biting, and whatever else she could do to get this drunken man off her. What made me so angry was when I learned that no one tried to help. The people in the bread store just watched and did nothing. Adriana found Shaunna outside the bread store, huddled in a ditch, crying. When Shaunna was able to find her voice, she confided to Adriana what awful thing had happened to her. The girl who was her dearest friend replied with, "Those things happen. You can't tell anyone, or you'll be in trouble."

The puzzle was beginning to make sense. I now understood the persistent thumb sucking, her poor social skills, and not wanting to go to church (the bread store was located not far from our church). She suffered for two long years, afraid to tell anyone, afraid that she had done something wrong, afraid that she wasn't pure anymore, afraid that God hated her for what had happened. Why hadn't I seen the signs? Why didn't I question Shaunna more thoroughly about her thumb sucking? Why wasn't I there to protect my baby? Guilt flooded every part of my aching body. I had to get word to Mark. I picked up the phone receiver. My hands were shaking as I dialed the twelve-digit number.

How heartbroken Mark would be over the news of Shaunna's attack! I silently prayed that the Lord would give me the words to say. The phone was ringing. "Alô," Mark answered in Portuguese. Oh, it was so good to hear his voice.

"Mark, hi it's me." I tried to keep my voice composed, but I knew it was no use. Before I could even get out my first sentence, I was crying and Mark knew something was terribly wrong.

"Dana! What's the matter?" I could sense the alarm in his voice. "Oh, Mark! Shaunna just told me that she was raped two years ago in Brazil. She was afraid to tell us until now. She thought she had done something wrong. She thought we would be mad at her."

How does a parent bare news like this? He was crushed to know that someone had hurt his precious baby girl. Shaunna is such a daddy's girl. Mark had two more weeks still to finish loose ends in Brazil. We talked more frequently by phone. In one of our conversations, Mark told me about how he had walked the streets in the neighborhood where the rape took place, wanting so desperately to find the man who had committed such a horrendous crime against his precious teenage daughter.

When Mark returned from Brazil, we took Shaunna to Cook Children's Hospital to see Dr. Lamb. She met with Shaunna to talk about her rape. Mark and I sat in another room, waiting to hear from the doctor. Dr. Lamb reappeared and took us to a quiet room. She then shared the details of Shaunna's rape. Mark and I were heartbroken, hearing how our precious daughter had been abused. I really thought that I would die right there in that room. Mark reached out for me, and we both began sobbing uncontrollably. I don't know how long we sat there and cried, holding onto each other. God's grace was so evident. Mark and I could feel His presence in that difficult time.

We went to church that night, knowing that we needed to be fed and comforted. I vividly remember sitting next to Mark, yet feeling so alone in my grief, when my thoughts were interrupted by a hug. The hug was not just a mere squeezing of the shoulders, but enveloped my whole being. It was a very comforting hug. Someone must have seen the sadness in my face. Oh, how I needed that hug! I turned around to tell that person how much the hug meant to me, but no one was there. How could that be? I knew that I wasn't imagining someone hugging me, for it was very real. Suddenly, chill bumps ran up and down my body. I whispered ever so quietly, "Thank you Jesus." In that precise moment, I knew that Jesus had just cradled me in His precious arms, comforting me with His marvelous grace in that dark, lonely part of my life.

Looking back, I now understand why the Lord chose to have Justin's Tourette's manifest itself in 1997, causing us to leave Brazil. Shaunna felt safe to reveal her hidden secret, one that she had buried deep within her heart for two years. Rape affects not only the victim but the family as a whole. Shaunna underwent therapy at Cook Children's PHP (Partial Hospitalization Program). The therapists were so encouraging. Mark and I were able to share our feelings with other parents through a support group hosted by Cook Children's Hospital. Because Shaunna had buried her rape for two years, she suffered from Post-Traumatic Stress Disorder and Anxiety and Panic Disorder.

When her anxiety attacks would come, she visualized me as her rapist. She would swat at the skeletons that she saw coming her way. She would crawl into a fetal position and cry out for me. I kept saying, "Honey, I'm right here in front of you!" When she looked at me, it wasn't me that she saw, but rather the drunkard who had taken her innocence away and destroyed her spirit. She was inconsolable. When she had no will to live and wanted to commit suicide, we went to the hospital, seeking someone to help her. The psychiatrist had her make a pact not to hurt herself. She agreed and chose two people to call on for help. One was my dear, sweet mother, and the other was one of our dear friends, Melissa Fernandez. We called on them many nights. Many times Shaunna sat in Melissa's driveway while Melissa ministered to her. I remember one day feeling so exhausted, that when we took Shaunna over to Melissa's home, she told Mark and me to go and have some coffee together and get away for a couple of hours. We sure needed that time. Besides my mom, dad, and Melissa being a great source of comfort for Mark and me, we also found great solace in our mission director's wife, Linda Raley. She called every day to find out how we were holding up. Just to know that people cared was very important to us. Readers, you may not always know what to say, but that's okay. You don't have to say anything. Just call. Be there for that loved one or dear friend. By not calling to just say, *I'm so sorry for what's happened* or *I'm sorry for the loss of your loved one*, your silence will convey a message of indifference. Justin too was deeply affected by the rape. He felt that he could also become a victim. He suddenly became afraid of everyone and everything. While staying at one of the mission houses, he was afraid to walk in the other room for fear that someone would be hiding in the room, ready to abuse him the way that Shaunna had been abused. None of us were sleeping very well.

Linda suggested that I call my doctor and get something to help me sleep. My doctor wrote a prescription for a sleeping pill and anxiety pill for Shaunna when she would have her panic attacks. I wondered if our lives would ever be happy again. Would we ever have our "old" Shaunna back? While trying to help Shaunna and Justin cope with this tragedy and at the same time trying to help ourselves be strong for both of them, the Lord must have known that we needed a good laugh.

He giveth power to the faint; and to them that have no might he increaseth strength (Isaiah 40:29).

CHAPTER NINE

LAUGHTER – THE HEALING MEDICINE

*I*n spite of the tragedy that had broken our hearts, we still needed to report to our supporting churches on our medical furlough. Have you ever just needed a good laugh? We did, and boy did we get one! To keep our housing costs down while on furlough, we opted to stay at a state park campground for fifteen dollars a night as opposed to spending fifty dollars for a hotel room. Seeing that our Grand Caravan was suitable for sleeping in, we thought it would be a great idea. We settled in on a shady area, perfect for setting up camp. The air smelled so clean and the stars were shining brightly. The camp showers were within walking distance and proved to be very well kept as camp showers go. I finished my shower first and waited for Mark and Justin so we could go grab a bite to eat. Shaunna decided to stay with my mom and dad while we traveled to a few of our churches. When Mark came around the corner from his side of the shower, he was trying to get the water out of his ear. Nothing seemed to work.

You know how you shake your head to one side to dislodge the water? Well, every time he did that, he would feel a weird sensation deep within his ear. He put pressure on his ear and the sensation would subside, but not for long. I was getting worried now. His ear was hurting and he felt like he was going to fall down from being so dizzy. We knew that something was wrong. He couldn't drive in his condition, so I drove our van to the nearby city about half an hour away. We finally pulled into the emergency entrance of the hospital. I was praying that it wouldn't be packed. It wasn't. Thank you, Lord! The doctor took one look into Mark's ear and stated that he had a fly lodged in his ear. *A fly?* Who would have thought? The doctor poured mineral oil in Mark's ear to kill the fly, then took some tiny forceps to remove the insect.

As he was removing the fly, I noticed the wingspan was enormous with bright colors. It was the largest, most colorful horse fly that I had ever seen. The doctor examined Mark's ear again and noted that the horse fly had also scratched Mark's eardrum. He asked Mark how long it had been since he had received a Tetanus shot. Apparently, it had been too long, because a Tetanus shot was ordered. We walked out of the hospital, $450.00 poorer. We could have cried, but it was better to laugh. Despite the cost, it was nice to have something to take our minds off the tragedy that rocked our close-knit family unit.

Recently, my mother-in-law, Becky Lawhorn, reminded me of our dryer hose experience on our medical furlough. Justin was twelve years old, the age of changing hormones. Our van didn't have back seat air-conditioning like they do today, so Justin would ask us to crank up the air in the front, where we would literally freeze to death. There had to be a better way of traveling on furlough or we would never survive the adolescent hormones. Mark thought of a solution. After the necessary adjustments, our van reminded me of *The Ghost Busters.* Mark's ingenuity paid off. He drove to the store and returned with a dryer hose and duct tape. I thought, *What in the world are you going to do with those items?* He came up with a brainstorming idea. The silver-coiled dryer hose was duct taped to one of the front vents. He ran the hose between the front seats, over the suitcases and eventually stopped at the seat that Justin was occupying. He then secured it all with duct tape. It wasn't conventional, but it sure did the trick. We were thankful not to be freezing to death, and Justin was glad to have the cold air cooling him off using the dryer hose invention.

CHAPTER TEN

FIELD CHANGE

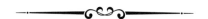

We tried to create some normalcy to our lives while going through such a dark valley. Justin was experimenting with some new medications that might help his Tourette's symptoms. He tried various combinations of drugs, but the only ones that worked for him were Effexor XR and Risperdone. The Effexor targeted his OCD symptoms and depression, while the Risperdone helped to lessen his tics.

The Lord in His infinite wisdom knew that returning to Brazil was not an option. We really had no clue as to what our lives would hold. Several pastors asked us to come and help them in their churches, but we felt that God still wanted us on the foreign field. We knew it needed to be where Shaunna and Justin's needs could be met, but where? The Lord already had a plan. We received word that missionaries from New Zealand and England were in need of someone to come and take care of their works while they took a much-needed furlough. We put a fleece out before the Lord: Whoever responded first to our letters of availability would be the country to which we would minister. The Lord is faithful. He answered our prayers.

New Zealand proved to be as beautiful as we had imagined. What was such a blessing was that Shaunna felt something she hadn't felt in a long time, safe. We were praising the Lord for still allowing us to minister on foreign soil. Shortly after our arrival in New Zealand,

Dale and Janet Brown took us to their son's cricket game (I still don't understand the sport), and then on to a fast food restaurant. When we were ready to order, Janet mentioned that she would *shout* for us. I thought, *why would someone want to shout for us?* Later, in the course of the meal, I asked Janet what she meant by *shouting* for us. "Oh," she said, "That means that we're going to pay for you." I thought to myself, *This is like learning a new language.*

I love the way the New Zealanders talk. It's so proper compared to the Texas slang. The British English was like learning a new set of vocabulary all over again. We just thought we knew English! I soon learned the terminology for the word *tea*. This little three-letter word can cause quite a bit of confusion if you're a Texas girl like me. *Morning tea* consists of a cup of hot tea and a few biscuits (that's what they call cookies). Actual biscuits, as you might imagine, are called scones. Years ago, my mom taught me how to make sourdough biscuits. I made a batch of these for a church function and presto – they were a hit with the Kiwi people. The beverage tea is never served cold, only hot with a little bit of cream or milk. The people grimaced when I told them that I like my tea poured over ice. They about flipped. *Afternoon tea* is what we would consider a mid-afternoon snack. If someone says, "Let's have tea," you'll know that they're inviting you over for supper – or is that dinner?

I grew up calling the evening meal *supper.* If you're from the south and someone calls you to have supper with them, then you might expect to eat something like chicken fried steak and mashed potatoes, (smothered in gravy), green beans, and a delicious apple crumb pie to finish off the meal. They too use the term *supper,* but the Kiwi people give this six-letter word a completely new meaning. It's not exactly what one would consider the evening meal. I invited some friends over for supper but was taken by surprise when they suggested coming over around 10:00 p.m. You guessed right. *Supper* is translated as a late night snack, around 10:30 or 11:00 p.m.

I learned very quickly that a serviette is a napkin. A *nappy,* which by the way sounds a lot like napkin, is a diaper; so don't ask the waitress for a napkin unless you want a diaper. *Spot on* means a good job. *Shivers* is another way of saying mercy. *Spitting* is the terminology used when it starts sprinkling outside. The polite word *restroom* is not understood in New Zealand, but bring up the word *toilet* or *the loo,* and they'll guide you in the right direction. If you're going to move, then you're *shifting.* One morning I decided to have a haircut. I mentioned to the hairdresser that I wanted to keep my bangs. She gave me an odd look, and I realized there must be another word for bangs. There is. They're called *fringes.* The only fringes that I've ever seen are the ones hanging from a fancy pillow. A friend is a *mate.*

While preparing for Sunday school, I thought, *We'll play the game tic-tack-toe. That will be fun for the kids to play, using Bible questions from the previous story.* You should have seen the look of surprise on their faces when I told them they were going to play the game tick-tack-toe. I asked for a show of hands for those who were familiar with the game. To my amazement, not a single hand lifted. I supposed they had never heard of the game. As I was arranging the X's and O's, I heard a faint gasp when all the children said in unison, "That's naughts and crosses!"

While fundraising for the young people, selling hot dogs at a sausage sizzle, a customer commented to me that he would take care of the *bloke* next to him. I was afraid to ask what that meant for fear that he might have been cussing him out. I found out that *bloke* is simply another word for *man.* If you're tired, then you're *shattered.* You don't call a taxi; you *order one.* You don't go to sleep; you *have a sleep.* If you want to check something out, you *have a look.* You don't *phone a friend,* you *ring* them. If a food or anything else is disgusting, then it's *revolting.* Last, but not least, if you're waiting for a particular event to happen, you're not excited; you're *rapt.* Here's a good one – if you're *under the weather,* you're *drunk.*

In June of 1998, we took care of Tom and Lisa Reesor's work in the city of Paraparaumu. They built a house on the church property some years ago, so we moved in and made their home our home for that first year. It was a beautiful, two-story home with three bedrooms and two baths. Mark even had his own study. Before the Reesors boarded the plane for furlough, we all stayed together for three weeks. It can get pretty hairy with two families living under the same roof, but we all made it through just fine. Lisa cooked the meals and I cleaned the kitchen. After they left for furlough, I pre-pared our first meal for our family. I couldn't seem to get the oven to work. I turned the knob to bake and made sure the temperature was set. I even turned the switch on the wall to the "on" position. I thought that maybe I had done something to the oven. Frantically, I called one of the women in the church. She came over and solved my dilemma. She directed my attention to the switch on the wall. I told her that I already turned that switch on. She informed me that I was used to the backward switches in the States. I learned quickly that to turn a switch on, whether it was an oven switch or light switch, I needed to flip the switch in the opposite direction of what I would normally do in the States.

The same held true for automobiles. To me, everything was back-wards in New Zealand. The steering wheel is located on the right side. Most cars are standard, so the gears are shifted with the left hand. The passenger sits where normally the driver would sit. I always felt like I was in a side car, trying to get into the van. One of the tricki-est moves was remembering which way the traffic went. Fortunately, the many times we turned the wrong way onto a street, no cars were coming our way.

I noticed that I felt tired most of the time, but passed it off as being due to my hysterectomy seven weeks prior to our arrival in New Zealand. Mrs. Moffit, Pastor B.R. Moffit's widow, told me that she would sell hysterectomies on the street corner if she could! I knew it would take about a year for me to fully recover. In the recovery room following my hysterectomy, I remember my pastor's wife, Sherry Moody, feeding me ice chips. The church people were so good to Mark and me. I had so many flower bouquets lining my hospital room. I noticed that my stomach continued to ache terribly. The doctors and nurses were positive that it was due to my surgery, but then shortly, I started running a fever. After the fever, came the vomiting and diarrhea. The doctor finally stated that I had the flu. Jokingly, I told him that I would have gladly just accepted the hysterectomy.

Two weeks into the country, we experienced youth winter camp. During the week of camp, Wednesday was set aside for a trip to Mt. Rupeu, an active volcano. It actually erupted back in 1996. There was such a diversity of people at camp – Fijians, Samoans, Cook Islanders, Philipinos, Australians, Maoris, and the Kiwis.

While getting settled into the Kiwi culture, we started looking for a doctor who could prescribe the necessary Effexor and Risperdone for Justin. We weren't real pleased with the doctor prescribing these medications for Justin, but we knew that at least she wouldn't be used as a counselor for him. We were disappointed to find out that Effexor XR wasn't available in New Zealand. I explained to the doctor that Justin could not take Paxil, because it made him very depressed. She said okay and prescribed a different medication for him, one I was not familiar with.

After a few days, I started noticing a difference in Justin's behavior and attitude. I became suspicious and looked up the chemical name of the medication on the Internet. Would you believe that she prescribed him Paxil? I was so angry. Mark and I needed to find some way of getting Effexor XR into the country. After two weeks of searching, we found a pharmacy that imported prescription drugs from Switzerland that normally couldn't be found in New Zealand. Mark and I were so thankful that Justin could continue on with his Effexor.

It was so hard adjusting to the culture of the Kiwi people. I learned that because of my friendliness, visitors didn't come back. The Kiwis are very cautious people. Every time we had visitors in the church, I would be outgoing with them and invite them back to the services. After the third week of visitors not returning, I knew that I was doing something wrong. I tried another strategy. When the visitors came, I acknowledged their presence but said no more about their return visit. I finally pushed the right button. Because I extended an invitation for them to return, they felt threatened and pressured to return. The hardest part of the non-Christian Kiwi culture was hearing the profanity that flowed from their mouths.

Some have asked, Does persecution exist in New Zealand? Maybe not like you might think, but in my opinion, it exists. I believe Justin suffered the most persecution. He loved roller blading at the local skateboard park. Two or three times a week the phone would ring with Justin on the other end. Talking just above a whisper, he would say, "Mom, can Dad come and pick me up? The boys from the park are waiting to beat me up." It wasn't unusual for him to come home with a bloody nose and bruises. Because the boys knew Justin was a Christian, they would antagonize him, trying to get him to swear, or they would make fun of his American culture and ridicule him for being an American. In spite of the snide remarks, he found the courage to share the Gospel with several of the boys. One boy confided to Justin that he decided to give church another try. Many times, I wish the Lord would allow us to see our future, but oh, how He knows what a mistake that would be for us! If we always knew our fate, then how could our faith be exercised?

Now faith is the substance of things hoped for, the evidence of things not seen (Hebrews 11:1).

This is my commandment, that ye love one another, as I have loved you (John 15:12).

CHAPTER ELEVEN

SHIRLEY AND SHEILA

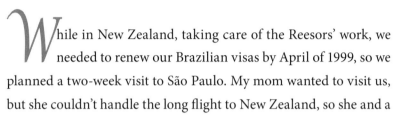

While in New Zealand, taking care of the Reesors' work, we needed to renew our Brazilian visas by April of 1999, so we planned a two-week visit to São Paulo. My mom wanted to visit us, but she couldn't handle the long flight to New Zealand, so she and a friend, Sheila Nelson, decided to fly to Brazil to spend some time with us. Mom and Sheila were able to acquire stand-by tickets through a friend on Delta Airlines. They flew from Dallas to Atlanta to connect to Brazil. Dallas was a breeze, but they hit a snag in Atlanta.

Mom and Sheila checked in promptly in the allotted time for stand-by passengers. The ticket agent in Atlanta took one look at my mom and stated to Sheila that she was free to board but the lady with her would have to change her appearance. My mom was puzzled as to why her clothing wasn't appropriate. She was wearing a sporty lavender, two-piece pantsuit with comfortable tennis shoes. The ticket agent kindly explained to Mom that she couldn't board the plane, because her blouse did not meet the standards for non-revenue ticket holders – *no collar.* A silent prayer was lifted to God in earnestness. As Mom prayed, God already had a plan. His divine plan came by way of a dear flight attendant. "Ma'am," she said quietly to Mom. "You can use this jacket of mine." God knows our needs even before we are aware of them. Mom thanked the kind woman and put on the much too-short long-sleeve collared jacket.

Sheila was already beginning to chuckle at Mom's appearance. You see, not only did the sleeves not quite reach Mom's slender wrists, but her short sleeve lavender blouse was much longer than the white short jacket provided by the lady. Now that Mom was ready to board, she once again approached the agent for her boarding pass. The agent made a quick inspection of Mom's attire and then paused. That pause concerned Mom and Sheila. Their thoughts were interrupted by the agent's sympathetic voice, "Excuse me ladies. I'm sorry, Ma'am, but your tennis shoes as well aren't appropriate for non-revenue. Do you have a pair of dress shoes in your carry-on bag?" Mom politely informed him that unfortunately she did not. She even checked with Sheila but no such luck. Mom was sure that she would be the cause for missing their long awaited flight. Where would she find dress shoes at the last minute? God in all His magnificence still had a plan.

Remember the kind flight attendant? She reappeared, and came to Mom's rescue by producing a pair of ballerina shoes. Mom took one look at them and knew immediately that they were way too small. She again thanked the flight attendant, discarded her own white thick socks, and proceeded to scrunch her toes in order for the seemingly tiny shoes to fit. Sheila was in stitches at the sight of Mom trying to walk to the desk for the agent's approval. As before, the agent quickly inspected Mom on her makeshift wardrobe. The agent agreed that Mom was just about ready to board, but one more thing was needed --a pair of hose --. Mom would have preferred wearing the tight fitting ballerina slippers bare-skinned without having to hunt down a pair of knee-high hose.

Mom was about to run to the nearest duty free shop or souvenir shop in hopes of finding some knee-high hosiery, but she didn't have to run far. In fact, she didn't have to run at all. Apparently, the flight attendant saw the panic in Mom's eyes and asked if she could help. Mom stated that hosiery was required to board the plane. The flight attendant simply responded with, "no problem." She handed Mom a pair of anklet stockings. Just as she donned the anklets and slippers, their flight number was called. They made their way to the ticket desk with Mom shuffling in the too-small ballerina slippers and Sheila beside herself with laughter at the sight of Mom. Let me paint you a word picture: Mom's lavender pant suit with the collarless blouse covering her hips, the short, white collared jacket that just comes to her rib area, and the too-small ballerina slippers with the anklet hosiery. No wonder Sheila couldn't keep from laughing! If that wasn't bad enough, the ticket agent took one look at Mom, leaned over to Sheila and sarcastically remarked that they could have gone first class if it hadn't been for her friend's appearance. They finally boarded the plane, laughing almost all the way to Brazil!

Mark thought we were in a war zone when we landed in São Paulo. Compared to New Zealand, it did look like a war zone. Justin loved being back in Brazil. His Portuguese came right back to him. It was as if he had never left. What a joy it was to see all of our friends again. We arrived a week before Mom and Sheila, which gave us time to acclimate to the climate and regain some of our Portuguese before they arrived. Shaunna didn't make the trip with us. She was attending the local high school in New Zealand and felt that she wasn't ready to return where the assault had occurred. We stayed with Jerry Lantz, our co-worker, in his two-bedroom duplex. Mark and I took Jerry's bedroom, while Jerry and Justin took his second bedroom. When Mom and Sheila arrived, they took the second bedroom and Justin and Jerry bunked downstairs on the couches. We turned Jerry's life upside down. Being single, he wasn't accustomed to sharing his home with five more people, but we all managed to live with one another for two weeks, and Jerry was a great host for us all.

This was Mom's second trip to São Paulo. On Mom's first trip to São Paulo in 1994, we lived in a modest two-bedroom duplex. On one particular Saturday, Mom was tired and suggested that she stay home to prepare our evening meal for us when we returned. What a great idea! What a treat for our meal to be ready for us when we got home.

Mom took a leisurely nap that day and then decided around half past four to start making the dinner preparations. I had already instructed her that the chicken was in the fridge, ready to be cooked. She was surprised when she found no canned goods lining the pantry. Then she remembered. Vegetables in cans didn't exist. Everything was made from scratch. When we finished our visitation and walked in the front door of our home, the aroma of fried chicken, homemade biscuits and cream gravy was mouthwatering. She said cooking from scratch took her back to her childhood days when she used to make baking powder and sourdough biscuits from scratch for what seemed to be an army of brothers and sisters. One thing's for sure. She never lost her touch. She's still as good a cook as ever.

I had the privilege of taking care of Mom in May of that same year. She was diagnosed with breast cancer with five lymph nodes positive. After her mastectomy, I was able to stay and care for her for six weeks. I loved being there, taking care of Mom and Dad's needs. I missed Mark and the kids, but it sure was nice to see my three sisters, Della Vaughan, Diane Links and Darlene Williams. Today, Mom is a cancer survivor and a great inspiration to everyone around her.

Mom and Sheila loved the way of the Brazilian people. We took them to Adelaide's two-room home to experience a traditional Brazilian meal. Adelaide, a widow of eight years, happily shares her small dwelling with her five grown children and three small grandchildren. Unbelievably, she built her concrete block home herself. Mom and Sheila were in awe at the feast set before their eyes. Beans, white steamed rice, pasta with marinara sauce, tender baked chicken, creamy potato salad and fresh cuts of cube steak, seasoned and fried in onion and garlic, graced this dear lady's small kitchen table. Guarana, a carbonated Brazilian favorite soft drink, was served as the beverage. The meal was topped off with a fruit salad, consisting of fresh pineapple, mangos, apples, bananas, papaya and a few dollops of whipped cream. The Brazilians loved Mom and Sheila. I know they look forward to seeing them again someday. It was hard saying good-bye to the people we loved, but at the same time we were looking forward to getting back to our people in New Zealand that the Lord had left in our care.

Casting all your care upon him; for he careth for you
(I Peter 5:7).

CHAPTER TWELVE

MISS LARDEN

When Tom and Lisa returned from furlough, we turned their home back over to them and made tentative plans to move thirty minutes down the coast to care for Dale and Janet Brown's work while they were on furlough in the States. After much prayer, we decided it was best to stay on the Kapiti coast. It would be much easier on Shaunna and Justin not to have to move to a new area and make new friends all over again.

We rented a beautiful three-bedroom brick home with a two-car garage. The yard was lovely with magnolias and pansies scenting the air with a glorious aroma. What was even better was the price of the rent, $500.00 U.S. dollars. One traffic light graced the small town. Outside our living room bay window sat the foothills nearby. How beautiful it was to see God's glorious creation.

Even though I loved New Zealand and the beauty it held, I was still in love with Brazil. Our prayer before we went to New Zealand was that the Lord would allow us, at some stage in our ministry, to return to our first love – *Brazil*. Mark and I both felt burdened about returning to our first love, but we weren't sure if it was God's leading or our own desire to be back there. We left it in God's hands, knowing that His will would be accomplished.

A few weeks later, we received an e-mail from our co-worker, Jerry Lantz, asking if there was a possibility of our returning to Brazil. That evening, Mark sent an e-mail to a pediatric neurologist in São Paulo asking if Brazil had any knowledge of Tourette's Syndrome. *In order for us to return to Brazil, Justin would need his medication, previously not available in any part of Brazil.* The next morning Mark checked the e-mail and found a letter from the neurologist stating that Brazil now had a Tourette's Syndrome Foundation and had the medications available if needed. My heart began to beat rapidly! Could it be true? Would we someday be able to return to Brazil? Mark sought counsel from our pastor and our mission director. We prayed for the next few weeks before making any concrete decisions. We felt in our hearts that God was giving the "okay" for us to return to our first love, Brazil. Shaunna had already made plans to attend Arlington Baptist College, so we felt that returning to Brazil was a definite possibility.

Justin's Tourette's was getting worse every day. It was in its full-blown stage. Adolescence will do that. There were days when he had no will to live. I vividly remember one such day that Justin and I were at home alone. His TS was over the edge that day. The "monster" living within him was too much to bear. He kept pleading for the rage to go away. Throughout the day, I prayed with him, calling on the Lord for strength and wisdom. While taking a load of clothes to the laundry room, I was terrified to see Justin holding a pocketknife so close to his throat. I called out, "Oh, God. Please help me to help Justin!" "Mom," he cried. "Please kill me. I want to be with Jesus!" I mustered up the strength to wrestle him to the ground and secure the knife in his sweaty palm. By now, we were both crying, exhausted. Satan, once again, was defeated. We prayed and thanked the Lord for His mercy and power.

One day while eating at a fast food restaurant, Justin commented that the employee wasn't using gloves to prepare the food. We thought it strange that he would pay any mind to the preparing of the food. For the next two years, Obsessive Compulsive Disorder (OCD) became a new part of Justin's battle with his Tourette's. His food could not be touched by bare hands. It was extremely difficult for him to eat out with us or to be eating with a large group of people.

At home, I used gloves when preparing or handling any food. During those two years of his food obsession, I couldn't touch or kiss him. On one particular day, I was making peanut butter cookies when Justin came into the kitchen. He reached for a pile of cookies. I instinctively reached for the cookies in his hands. As I did, my hands touched his hands. He ran from the room crying in a rage. I ran after him, apologizing for touching his hands. I always tried to remember not to touch his skin, but sometimes I just honestly forgot. I told him that dinner was just about ready and that the cookies would ruin his appetite. After his hour-long rage, he came out of his room exhausted, crying, "Mom, I'm sorry. Please don't hate me." I assured him that I didn't hate him, but that I loved him very much. Mark and I were both trying to understand this new part of Justin's TS. I asked him what would happen if I hugged him, kissed him, or touched his food with my bare hands. He stated that he would surely die.

Justin needed a psychologist, one that was a Christian and knew something of Tourette's Syndrome. Through phone calls that led us from one counselor to another, we finally found Miss Larden. We scheduled a consult to see how compatible she and Justin would be. Justin liked her immediately. She was twenty-three years old, had a great rapport with Justin and best of all – specialized in Tourette's and OCD. After each daily session, she reminded Justin that Satan was lying to him. Each week, Miss Larden gave Justin a new challenge that would bring him closer to overcoming the oppression of his OCD.

Mark and I prayed fervently and earnestly that Justin would have victory over Satan's hold upon his life. I knew that Satan was working overtime to hinder the ministry that God had planned for Justin's life. Adults and children were coming to know Christ as their Savior, which meant God's angels were rejoicing, but Satan's army was on the warpath. We trusted God that Justin would have the victory over his OCD. How long could we endure Satan's grip on Justin's life? Could we survive this dark valley? By God's grace we did, taking each day to God in prayer.

CHAPTER THIRTEEN

ANOTHER VALLEY

Youth retreat camp was just around the corner. July of 2000 proved to be as cold as the weatherman had predicted. The seasons are opposite in New Zealand. Excitement filled the air as campers were chatting away as to whom would be at camp that year, what skits would be performed, and so on. They all looked forward to seeing friends they hadn't seen in a year's time. During that week of camp, six precious young people committed their lives in total surrender to the Lord. What a joy it was to see the change in those young people's lives. Seven churches were represented that year with an attendance of around one-hundred and fifty campers. Saying goodbye is never easy to new friendships made, knowing that most likely you won't see those friendly faces for at least another year. As I said my goodbyes to the pastors' wives, a tiredness consumed my body that I dismissed as *after camp overload.*

I gave my tired body a chance to recuperate from the hectic but rewarding week. However, my body didn't bounce back as I had hoped. I decided the best plan was to make an appointment with my primary care doctor. I expressed to my doctor that my eyes felt very tired. He inquired if anyone in my family suffers from Thyroid disease. When I mentioned that my mother suffers from low Thyroid, he ordered a blood test to determine if that was the cause for my unexplained inability to regain my strength. Knowing that Thyroid problems run in my family, I was sure that was to be the case for me. A week later, I received word that all my tests came back normal. His diagnosis? – a probable virus that would pass in a few days. I wasn't convinced, but because blood tests don't lie, I resigned myself to double up on my vitamins and get some extra sleep to ward off this strange feeling virus.

Little did I know that I was about to enter yet another valley that would not only test my family's faith but would test my own as well. Isaiah 43:2, 3 would prove to be my life's verse. Indeed, Mark and I would go through the flooded waters and the burning fires, despite our futile efforts to find a way out of the valley that we were to endure, yet it was all in His divine plan. The Lord whispered to me, *Be still and know that I am God.* God was in control of whatever was happening to my body. What wonderful promises we have from the Lord that He will carry us through our trials and take us to the mountaintop.

Mark and I were assured that some rest would do me good, so we decided to spend a couple of days in Hastings, a beautiful resort area located on the western part of the North Island. We packed our car for the 5-hour drive. I was really looking forward to some relaxing days. Hot mineral pools and natural springs make this small town so enticing. Trees with blooming red buds lined the neat, clean streets. Hotels are like none I've ever seen. When we called for reservations, the receptionist wanted to know if we wanted a one or two-bedroom suite. Naturally, we requested a two-bedroom. They are a one-floor dwelling equipped with a kitchenette, a living area, and two complete bedrooms with a bathroom adjoining the two rooms. The patio, adjacent to the living room, opened to the most invigorating mineral pool. What a delight it was to soak in the hot pools, especially since it was wintertime in July. God is so good to His children!

The mineral pools situated in the hub of the city could easily lull one to sleep with the calm and peaceful captivating music. Tea lights danced merrily as the water reflected their beauty. The foggy water was extremely hot, but oh so soothing to my tired muscles. That week in Hastings proved to be what I needed, for I could feel my body regaining its strength.

Over the course of the next few weeks, I noticed something awry with my eyes; they would squint ever so slightly when people talked to me. To be perfectly honest with you, it was quite embarrassing. I guess the most embarrassing times were in church. Once the singing and preaching started, my eyelids would slowly close. I can just imagine what everyone thought about the missionary wife – there she goes again, falling asleep in church. I tried everything to keep my eyes open. Finally I had to raise my eyelids by using my index fingers. This was the only way that I was able to watch the service.

When friends came to our house, they would urge me to lie down. They said I looked so tired, but after those relaxing days in Hastings, I didn't feel very tired. I started noticing that when I walked, my eyelids would immediately shut, causing me to stop right in my tracks. I thought, *What is happening to me?* I was nervous, scared and discouraged all at the same time, not knowing what was wrong with me. Then I asked myself, *Is there really anything wrong with me, or is it just in my head? No!* I talked back to myself. *There is something wrong; I just have to find out what it is.* I was consumed with frustration because of my inability to care for my family. Because our primary care doctor was clueless to my condition, Mark and I took it upon ourselves to investigate the reasons for my eyes not being able to stay open.

The following week, Mark and I met with a local optometrist, hoping to find some answers to whatever was happening to me. He did a vision screen test and everything was normal. Every test he performed came back negative. What now? I think he was just as baffled as we were. I began describing to him in detail about my eyes closing when

I walked, watched TV, listened to the radio or really performed any task. He thought it might be a communication problem. Just then, he commented to Mark that he noticed something unusual about my eyes. He noted that when I talked, my eyes opened just fine, but when he talked to me, my eyes would slowly close. It was then that I realized he was exactly right. To make sure of his findings, he tested me. He would talk, and then I would talk. Sure enough, when he made any audible sound, my eyes would close, but when I spoke, my eyes amazingly opened without any help. He suspected that something neurological was malfunctioning, so he suggested we visit a neurologist. That was a difficult task. How would we know which specialist to visit? There's something about being in a foreign country and trying to find the right doctor to treat a neurological problem. Mark made a few phone calls, and we decided on a doctor in the Wellington area.

The city of Wellington is nestled among the rugged foothills at the southern tip of the North Island. Taking the winding road that overlooks the Tasman Sea, it took us about an hour to drive from our home on the Kapiti Coast to a Dr. Fung in Wellington. In the hour drive to this beautiful city, all kinds of questions were running through my mind. *What could my problem be? Is there a name to what I have? Is it fatal? Is there a cure? Is there really anything wrong with me?* A few days prior to my visit with Dr. Fung, I was cleaning out the refrigerator when one of my magnets caught my eye. *Trust in the Lord with all thine heart...* (Proverbs 3:5). The tears began to flow. Had I been fully trusting the Lord? I poured out my frustrations and worries to the Lord. He comforted me as only He can. What a joy it is to have sweet fellowship with our Lord and Savior. What a relief it is to know that our Lord and Savior is with us no matter what we go through. He promised me that I would never walk alone. I may *feel* at times that I'm drowning in my valleys, but God promised me that I would not drown and that He would be with me every step of the way.

We were sitting in the neurologist's office, hoping to find some answers. Dr. Fung did all the standard neurological tests and found that everything was in order. He ordered a MRI to rule out any tumors or legions on the brain stem. He felt there could possibly be a tumor of some kind pressing on my optic nerve. A tumor? I never gave any thought about the possibility of a tumor causing these problems. My sweet Jesus gently whispered, *Dana, remember to trust me.* My strength to press on was made strong by Mark's spiritual leadership in our home. Mark read inspirational passages from the Bible that helped me with my anxieties. *Be Anxious for Nothing,* was our verse to remember during those days of frustration. He is always in control of any situation. One of Mark's messages spoke directly to my heart. I like to call it the five P's of life. There is not a *Promise* that God cannot keep, There is not a *Problem* God cannot solve, There is not a *Pain* that God cannot comfort, There is not a *Person* that God cannot save, and There is not a *Path* that God cannot guard. The illustration that Mark gave in the end about peace still leaves me in awe of God's peace, grace and mercy. God is still on the throne, and He is able!

While waiting for a date to have the MRI, I noticed that my eyes were progressively worsening. I no longer had the ability to drive, enjoy a leisurely walk on the beach (walking would shut down my eyes), watch my favorite TV show without holding my eyelids up, bake goodies for my family or go grocery shopping alone. I felt like my independence was slowly being taken away from me, piece by piece. Mark had taken on my tasks of the cooking, cleaning, shopping, washing, home schooling and whatever else needed to be done. Shaunna and Justin chipped in and did all they could after their schoolwork was finished. Both were holding down jobs as well. Shaunna worked at Burger King, and Justin worked in the deli at the local supermarket. I felt totally helpless, but I was determined that Satan would not have the victory in my life.

The slightest whisper caused my eyes to close. I started finding tricks to open my eyes. When I wiggled my nose, my eyes would pop open. I joked that I felt like I was a guest on *Bewitched,* only I didn't go anywhere! I even found that my eyes would pop open when I drank a carbonated drink. I know it must sound strange to you, for it surely sounded strange to me. We sure got a barrel of laughs from the *tricks* that would open my eyes.

The day finally arrived for the MRI test. I've never had a test like that before. It was strange being in that cramped space. The loud clanging noises were somewhat frightening, but I made it through with excellence. It would take several days for an answer. Those few days of anticipation were torturous, jumping at the sound of the phone ringing, hoping it was news from the doctor. Word finally came. No tumors were found. We were praising the Lord over the news of no tumors, but now were left grappling with what could be wrong with me.

For a while, I felt as though it was all in my head. Was I dealing with a habit that I could control? I knew in my heart that it wasn't. I knew that something was definitely wrong with my eyes. Every week I noticed that it became harder for me to keep my eyes open at the slightest noise or the slightest step that I made. My neurologist prescribed some anti-seizure medicine to see how that might help. He was just as confused as we were, so we knew he was grasping for straws with the medicine.

In the meantime, Mark persistently searched the Internet to find a reason for my spasms. He found two major eyelid disorders: Myasthenia Gravis and Blepharospasm. Mark read aloud the information about Blepharospasm. My heart started beating rapidly. I thought out loud, "Hey! That's me! They're talking about me! I knew that something was wrong!" I could barely wait to tell my doctor what Mark had discovered on the Internet. I was surprised that my doctor hadn't already mentioned what I could possibly have. I continued taking the anti-seizure medicine but finally discontinued it, because it made me feel so sick.

Dr. Fung finally concluded that he had no idea what my problem was. Mark asked about the possibility of it being one of the two eyelid disorders that he had downloaded off the Internet. The doctor skimmed over the papers about the disorders. He dismissed both with a wave of his hand. Because my eyelids had good tone and were very taut, he ruled out the possibility of Myasthenia Gravis. He wasn't convinced of it being Blepharospasm either. He suggested that we wait until we returned to the States to find more answers.

For the next few weeks we continued to live our lives as normally as possible. Since we had scheduled our furlough far in advance of the eyelid problem, we continued with our plans to be back in the States before the semi-annual meeting of the World Baptist Fellowship. I had so hoped to find an answer to what was wrong with me, but then I remembered the inscription on the magnet, "TRUST IN THE LORD."

As the weeks crept by ever so slowly, the spasms worsened. I was only able to see the floor through a tiny slit in the bottom of my eyelids. In order to see other people talking, I would lean my head back and watch them through the slit in my eyelids. When I walked, the only thing visible to me was the person's shoes. I checked with Mark every day to see which shoes he was wearing. Mark's shoe style must have been very popular, because I found myself reaching out for "my man's hand," but it wasn't my man, just a stranger who found it odd that this crazy woman was trying to hold his hand.

When the Browns returned from furlough, their oldest son, Joshua, decided to change his hairstyle. After the Sunday morning service, I approached Joshua and commented on how nice his hair looked. He smiled warmly and said, "Thank you." He recounted the story to his mom, Janet, about how funny it was that the only person who noticed the change in his hairstyle was the "blind" lady in the church.

God's grace carried me through when I felt I had no strength to go on. I'll always treasure the friendships made in New Zealand. Those friendships helped to keep me spiritually strong while battling something I thought had no name or even existed.

> Fear thou not; for I am with thee: be not dismayed; for I am thy God: I will strengthen thee; yea, I will uphold thee; yea, I will uphold thee with the right hand of my righteousness (Isaiah 41:10).

CHAPTER FOURTEEN

THE MIRACLE

*I*t was October of 2000 when we boarded the plane bound for the United States. Mark was swift in scheduling an appointment for me to see a neurologist. The earliest date available wasn't until October 20th. By now, my eyes were completely shut. I later learned that I was "functionally blind." I wore dark sunglasses to avoid the embarrassment of curious onlookers. There are so many things we take for granted; namely, our sight. Walking was very difficult. Even though Mark told me there wasn't anything I could trip on, I still wasn't confident that I wasn't going to fall. In my sub-conscious, I pictured myself running into a wall or tripping over a curb. Even though I knew that Mark would tell me of any obstacles in my way, I found it hard to totally trust his guiding arm. It's ironic how we treat our Lord the very same way.

Eating out was just as much of a challenge. I recall eating at one of my favorite Mexican restaurants, when I suddenly had the urge to use the restroom. The distance from our table to the restroom was just a few short feet, but for me it was miles away. I was embarrassed to ask Mark to lead me to the restroom, so I sat in my chair contemplating my strategy of getting to the restroom. I was concentrating so hard on willing my eyes to open that I could feel the pulling of my neck muscles and felt the strain of the muscles in my collarbone area. Do you have any idea what muscles a person uses to open their eyes? I didn't until I had to use my neck and collarbone muscles to make my eyes function. Well, needless to say, I didn't get to the restroom that day, for fear of looking strange in front of other people.

The semi-annual meeting of the World Baptist Fellowship was two weeks away. I have always looked forward to those meetings with excitement and anticipation. My excitement was slowly fading, and anxiety filled every part of my being. How would friends that I hadn't seen in over ten years react to my situation? At first it was very difficult to accept everyone's pity, but then I realized that it wasn't pity at all, but love, sympathy and concern. People would come up to me and say, Hello, Dana, this is so and so. Everyone was just wonderful. Sometimes my eyes would just suddenly pop open. It was hilarious. On one occasion, a good friend of ours, Larry Brundige, was describing how fit and handsome he was. At that precise moment, my eyes popped open and I was able to reveal to him how he had acquired "love handles" and was slightly gray. Isn't the Lord good!

At the end of services, Mark and I went down to pray at the altar for God's healing and grace. It felt so good to pour my heart out to Him. What a wonderful service it was. Sleep came that night, and I had peace in my heart. On the second day of our meeting, Mark and I met with the panel of men who make up the mission committee for our mission board. Because we were making a move from New Zealand back to Brazil, we needed to discuss it with the men. At the end of our discussion, one of the pastors, Rick Austin, recommended that all of the men lay hands on Mark and me and pray that my sight might be renewed. Mark and I were so moved by the inspirational and heart-felt prayer of the committee members. I wonder how many of us that day in that small room were expecting a miracle that was already on its way.

It had been a good day at the meeting! On our way home, Mark and I were pondering the messages that fed our souls, and the fellowship that lifted our spirits. As I was commenting on one of the messages, my eyes started flickering. It was a strange sensation. I thought it odd at first, but then I remembered the prayer of those mighty men of God. I had chill bumps running up and down my arms. "Mark!" I cried. "Look at my eyes! I can see! I can really see!" Mark stole a glance at me while driving and couldn't believe what he was seeing. He pulled over to the shoulder of the road, stopped the car, and gathered me in his arms. We were holding each other, crying, and thanking God for his mercy on my life. My eyelids were functioning normally. I didn't have to strain the least to lift my eyelids. There was no headache. There was no neck pain. My eyelids felt as light as a feather. I could see the road in front of us. I could see the train carrying its contents to the next town. I could see. I couldn't wait to show everyone at the meeting what miracle God had performed in my life.

I still remember the look of surprise as I walked through the door of the meeting that night – *with my eyes open*. People ran up to me crying, overcome with emotion that a real live miracle had taken place. People were crying out, "Praise the Lord", "Hallelujah," "Amen." The committee members were all whooping and hollering! I guess that's what you call a *"Bapticostal"* fit. We were all laughing and crying at the same time. I could feel the power of God throughout the entire meeting.

On the very night of my miracle, the mission committee members expressed their thanks to God and called out for Mel Neil, missionary to Ecuador, to come to the altar. Mel was suffering from a cancer that was slowly taking over his body. The mission committee members, along with the men of the church, asked God for another miracle as they laid hands on Mel, praying for divine healing. Mel and Charlene

Neil have a vital ministry today of sending needed Bibles to foreign fields, all because of some men who didn't just stop at one miracle. What a great and mighty God we serve. After the conference, my eyes went back to their *blind* state, but what a blessing it was to share that experience with those who earnestly prayed for God's divine healing.

Once the conference was over, we began looking for an apartment to rent. Mark and I weren't sure what would happen with my eye situation, so staying in the mission house over a long period of time was out of the question. Justin desired to try public school, which led us to the Mansfield School District. The apartments really were not in our budget but were in one of the safer areas of town. It had been ages since we had paid more than $600.00 in rent. The tiny two-bedroom Mansfield apartment cost us a bundle – $815.00 each month, excluding any utilities. It was difficult, but I wouldn't have traded it for anything. I loved the privacy. It would have been hard to share a house with others. I felt so safe in our little apartment. To go outside was a major chore for me. I just wanted to crawl in bed and stay there – forever. I had never dealt with that feeling before. As long as I was in our apartment, I was fine. When I knew that I needed to leave the house for any reason, my heart would start beating fast, and the palms of my hands would sweat dreadfully. I had to talk myself through the ordeal of leaving our "safe" apartment.

Mark had once again taken on my tasks of the household duties. The clothes came out clean and fresh smelling. The meals were delicious. The apartment was kept in order and even the home schooling records were kept up-to-date. Mark is my knight in shining armor. Not once did he ever complain about the double shift he pulled – his workload as well as mine.

Call unto me, and I will answer thee, and show thee great and mighty things, which thou knowest not (Jeremiah 33:3).

CHAPTER FIFTEEN

LOOKING FOR ANSWERS

O n October 30, Mark and I were sitting in the office of neurologist, Dr. McMichael, hoping to get some answers about why I couldn't keep my eyes open. Because I couldn't see, Mark was asking me all the questions on the form, and I was answering them to the best of my knowledge. I knew there were other people in the waiting room. That really unnerved me. I just knew they were all staring at me, wondering what was wrong with me. I could feel my cheeks warming from the embarrassment I faced from not being able to open my eyes. Because I wasn't quite focused on the questions, Mark had to repeat some of them a few times. He was so patient with me.

When Dr. McMichael entered the room, I was praying that this would be the man that God used to find a cure for me. He ran the same kind of diagnostic tests that were done in New Zealand, only this doctor keyed in on something written in my file. He realized that Tourette's Syndrome, a neurological disorder that involves involuntary movements and sounds, runs in our family. He felt like he had the answer to my predicament. His diagnosis: I had Tourette's. I respectfully disagreed with the doctor. Mark and I have been studying Tourette's Syndrome for the past fourteen years, and I just felt like this possibly be the answer. He was so adamant about it that we agreed to see a movement specialist at the Baylor Medical Center in Dallas, Texas.

The next day, October 31, we were talking to the specialist in Dallas, wondering what his diagnosis would be. After extensive exams, he too keyed in on what was written in my file about our kids having Tourette's. When I questioned him about the possibility of my problem being Blepharospasm, a rare eyelid disorder that causes spasms of the eyelid muscles, he just kind of sloughed it off and said that it could be but most likely not. Just to make sure, he recommended a round of Botox injections. Botox is a highly purified form of the toxin, Botchollism. I agreed and came back the following day for treatment. I asked the all-too-familiar question; "Will it hurt?" He answered with, "You'll only feel a prick." By the time the fifth injection was injected into my eyelid, I felt as though I was going to die. The pain was just too much to bear. I was crying and screaming at the same time. He suggested we stop there and see how the shots worked.

I felt jittery for the next few days. My body had been through a very traumatic experience. I noticed that my left eye opened completely; while my right eye was open just a slit. Mark had been instructed by the doctor to tape my eyes closed at night, so they wouldn't dry out from floating open during the middle of the night. For the next six weeks, Mark taped my eyes closed each night. (I felt like I could pass for The Lone Ranger). The shots were supposed to be effective for about three months, but by the sixth week the shots had already worn off. He wanted to inject more of the Botox before Christmas. I was willing to try it again, for I wanted so badly for my eyes to be open for the Christmas holidays. Oh, how I longed to bake an apple pie or a home-cooked meal for my family.

It's usually not recommended injecting Botox at intervals sooner than 3 or 4 months. We figured this was a trial-and-error procedure, so we went ahead with his suggestion. I was already feeling the anxiety of the last time I had the shots. Two days before the shots, I received an e-mail from a dear friend of mine, Shaunna Smith. She prayed a prayer for me that God would heal me. I called her and told her of my upcoming shots. She prayed and cried with me over the phone.

Once again, I found myself lying on the table, sweating from fear, knowing how painful the shots would be. The doctor asked if I had any questions. I nodded and explained how I read about some special glasses called a *ptosis crutch* that hold the eyelids up. He nodded that he was aware of them but had no idea how to acquire them. He wasn't even sure if they still existed.

With the questions out of the way, the doctor asked if I was ready to proceed. He said the dosage needed to be stronger, so I knew the pain would be harder to endure. The Lord was with me the whole time. Mark was holding my hand as I lay there screaming in pain. The doctor was trying to soothe me with comforting words. I knew it would be over soon, but it felt like an eternity. The doctor informed us that if the shots didn't work, then it most likely was not Blepharospasm.

Ask, and it shall be given you; seek, and ye shall find; knock, and it shall be opened unto you (Matthew 7:7).

CHAPTER SIXTEEN

PRECIOUS MEMORIES AND TERRIFYING MOMENTS

*F*or the time that we were living in the apartment, Shaunna was attending the Arlington Baptist College and living in the girls' dorm. I remember my days at ABC and have such fond memories. I arrived at ABC as a young 17-year-old. I lived at home, commuting back and forth to the school. I made so many friendships. We wanted Shaunna to have those same wonderful experiences. I was secretly hoping that she would audition for one of the singing groups.

Mark and I sang and traveled with *The Ambassadors*. Our lives were forever changed from the fatal accident of October 1979. We were headed home from an engagement in Palestine, Texas. Amy Blue, our pianist, sang, "Home Where I Belong." Whenever Amy walked into a room, her presence lit the room. She always reminded me of an angel. Everyone in the group got along so well. We were like brothers and sisters. A mile from our exit in Grand Prairie, Texas, one of the tires on the van blew. At the same time, another tire blew. According to an eyewitness to the accident, the van flipped three times in midair, landed and scraped the ground before landing on the guardrail. An hour before the Grand Prairie exit, Amy and I had decided to change seats. I took the very back seat and she took my place in the first front long seat. I must have dozed, oblivious to the dangers that lie ahead. I remember waking up right before the accident and thinking to myself, "Oh, no, we're going to crash!" The van was swerving from one side of the lane to the other. Apparently, I was knocked unconscious, because I never felt the injury to my right forearm as it scraped the pavement when the van flipped and hit the ground hard. I was hospitalized for a week with serious injuries. Our director, Larry Brundige, broke several bones, including his neck, and was never expected to walk or sing again. The Lord had other plans for him. After surgery and months of therapy, he was not only walking again but was singing as well, using his beautiful talent for the Lord. I look forward one day to seeing my dear friend, Amy Blue, a young girl who touched so many lives with her sweet and quiet spirit.

While Shaunna was attending ABC, her Tourette's symptoms were making it hard for her to focus on school. We talked it over with her doctor and suggested that maybe a prescription of Prozac might be helpful. It seemed to help her stay focused in the beginning, but it really made it hard for her to get to classes on time. She was working at a local pet shop, so her schedule was full. I think that putting her on Prozac was probably not one of our wisest decisions. After one semester, she realized that she couldn't keep up with the demands of school and work while taking the Prozac. She moved in with relatives and worked at a supermarket nearby. The demands of trying to fit into the American culture had taken its toll on her. We decided to go ahead with our furlough, feeling that Shaunna would be okay with her new job. We arrived in Atlanta, Georgia, only to hear the next day that Shaunna had attempted suicide by taking an overdose of her Prozac. My mom called me with the bad news and told us that they would take her home with them after she was released from the hospital. We continued on with our furlough, not sure if our missionary days on foreign soil had come to an end.

Two weeks later, we arrived back in town and found a Christian counselor for Shaunna. Our insurance policy only allowed a cap of $1000.00 for mental health. Those funds were quickly absorbed by the high cost of premiums and out-of-pocket expenses. The summer of the following year, Shaunna expressed a desire to work at the Minnetonka Christian Camp. Mark and I both felt that this would be a great opportunity for her. Before we left for the road again, we visited her at Minnetonka and saw that she was adjusting very well.

On one particular night at camp, Shaunna had a flashback of her rape. A familiar sound or scent brought her back to that dreadful night. She was upset and impulsively took an overdose of a new medication that she was taking. Immediately after taking the pills, she called us on our cell phone to say goodbye and that she loved us. We were in church at the time of her call, so the answering machine picked up her message. After services I checked my phone and noticed that it read – *one missed call.* As I listened to the message, I instinctively knew that something was wrong when I heard Shaunna's voice on the other end.

I quickly called the camp and asked to speak to Shaunna. She came to the office phone and was crying, saying, "Mom, I'm sorry. Please don't be mad at me. I took an overdose of 92 pills." I told her that we were on our way to the camp. I quickly informed the camp workers of the situation at hand. We knew we had at least a five-hour drive ahead of us. The camp called an ambulance, and she was rushed to the Indian hospital so they could pump her stomach before all the contents of the pills were able to penetrate her stomach lining. We didn't know what lay in store for Shaunna or for us. I was crying and asking the Lord to have mercy on Shaunna's life and to bring her through this attempted suicide. She was moved to a county hospital a few hours away, where she was put into intensive care. Mark and I were able to stay in a Ronald McDonald House right across the street from the hospital. The Lord was so good to give us that place to stay while Shaunna was recovering.

The following week, she voluntarily entered a program for suicide and drug problems at a local hospital. She stayed there for a week, interacting with the other patients through group therapy. We also received family counseling to help Shaunna as well as ourselves to get through this difficult time in our lives.

Another year passed and things seemed to be going well for Shaunna. She was working and enjoying life again. As with any tragedy, life is never the same, and that was the way it was for Shaunna. She was continually receiving counseling, trying to get a grip on life. We knew that Shaunna was safe in the therapy program where she couldn't hurt herself. The thing that really saddens me is the fact that most people don't know how to deal with suicide attempts. It scares them. Shaunna needed more than her family to visit her in the hospital. She needed the support of friends. I know her friends were thinking of her, but they never came to visit her. True, it can be scary visiting a psychiatric ward, but it's important for Christians to realize that mental health issues are a very real problem in our society today. Having mental health problems doesn't make a person strange or weird. It just means that they need to talk out their problems more and maybe incorporate medicine into their daily struggles of life.

Shaunna's third and last suicide attempt caused our world to come crashing down around us. She became very depressed and impulsively took an over-the-counter pain medication. She reacted immediately and called my parents to let them know what she had done. I think the reason for her depression was the fact that she was renting a one-room apartment and was living by herself. My dad jumped into his truck and made the thirty-minute drive in about fifteen minutes.

Shaunna opened the door for him, and he held her in his arms. I think she was waiting for a scolding but only received love and comfort. I'm so thankful that I have parents who have always been there for Shaunna in her time of need.

God is our refuge and strength, a very present help in trouble (Psalm 46:1).

CHAPTER SEVENTEEN

SEARCHING FOR A CURE

*D*epression. Is it a sin for a Christian to be depressed? I don't consider myself a depressed person, but I *felt* depressed. Depression has many faces: loss of appetite, insomnia, lack of concentration, too much sleep, nausea, and many more. Could it be that I was depressed? Probably so. A spark of determination ignited my insides. I was determined to fight the dark cloud of depression that ominously threatened to destroy my desire to live for my Lord and Savior. I wanted to share God's amazing grace with all of our churches.

Mark always knows my needs. As of December 27, 2005, we had been married for twenty-five years, and he can just about read my mind. I always had the option to stay at home with Justin while Mark traveled on furlough, but I loved Mark taking care of me, so I opted to travel with him whenever I had the chance. Justin decided that he too would probably do better returning to homeschooling. His grades were dropping, and he wanted to make good scores, especially through his high school years. Probably the hardest part of traveling on the road was the bathroom stops. Usually we'd stop at rest areas, but that stopped as soon as I ran into a lady going out of the restroom. She was not sympathetic at all and even made a remark to that effect. I was crying, upset that people could be so rude. Mark assured me that everything would work out. He vowed that we would not use rest areas if we didn't have to, and we would stick to convenience stores, where there was only one bathroom. That way I wouldn't bump into anyone, and he could be there for me in case I needed anything.

Another area of anxiety was going to the churches. Don't get me wrong. The pastors and members were just wonderful to me. I think Satan was trying very hard to discourage me to just quit the ministry. I love to sing, and I feel that it's a ministry that God has given to me. I knew that if I gave in just one bit to Satan, I would be defeated. I remembered God's promise not to take us through more than we can bear, so I knew that apparently I was able to bear this affliction. When it was time for me to sing, I would quietly pray that God would help me to be a blessing to someone in the church. Mark would gently lead me on to the platform and afterwards help me down with such care. I felt so self-conscious about what *they* must think, but then Lucy Swindoll's words came to me about the people she labeled as *they* in our lives. She named them the *"royal they"*. They keep us from being obedient to God's will. Remember, God doesn't ask us to be successful, just obedient. When we are obedient to God, we will be successful.

The shots wore off sooner this time, and I vowed never to go through that pain again. I went back to Dr. McMichael, and he suggested I try Paxil, a drug that treats Tourette's symptoms. He was still leaning towards Tourette's Syndrome as my problem. I agreed to take the tiny pink pill that night. The next morning we left for Florida and I noticed that I felt different, a weird different. I felt very depressed inside. I had no energy. Later that day, I noticed that my face had broken out in a rash. I knew then that Paxil was not for me. After our return from Florida, I decided that I wanted to see some other doctors. I visited an ophthalmologist who impatiently told me that I had nothing more than droopy eyes. How could he be so inconsiderate? He was so rude and hateful. When I asked him about an apparatus called a *potosis crutch* for eyeglasses, he just kind of grunted and told me that was the biggest joke he'd ever heard. I left feeling defeated and worn out. It seemed that no one knew what was wrong with me.

Mark was determined to find an answer to my problem. Again, we visited another ophthalmologist in Dallas. All kinds of vision screen tests were done. I knew that it wasn't my vision, but I let them do their job anyway. They tested me for dry eyes, talking amongst themselves that this was truly my problem. The tests came back negative except for the dry eyes. My eyes were very dry but not severe. The doctor was very nice but had no news that we wanted to hear. He had no clue as to what was wrong with me. He said as much to Mark and that's all it took. Mark was so tired of hearing, "I'm sorry, I don't know what is wrong with your wife."

Mark bore his heart to the doctor of how he was so tired of hearing that no one knew what to do for me. The doctor sat and listened patiently as Mark spoke of his frustrations in trying to find an answer. Finally, the doctor said, "Mark, frustration is good, but not too much frustration. Frustration will get things done." We re-visited Dr. McMichael, who then proceeded to run some other tests on me. He was just as baffled as we were, but he was determined to find some answers for us. He ran a series of muscle tests. Those were extremely painful, but I was able to endure the pain through God's grace and the presence of Mark by my side.

The tests revealed that I had some muscle tension in my neck, so I had a MRI done, which revealed that I had some spurs on my spine, but nothing that needed surgery or would cause this problem to my eyes. When Dr. McMichael received word of the MRI, he told Mark and me that he would send us to the top specialists in the world to try to find out what was wrong with me. We appreciated his enthusiasm to find an answer for me. He said he would send me to the best doctor in the United States. He contacted two of them who were specialists in neurology. One was in Houston and the other in New York. We opted for Houston, seeing it was only a five-hour drive from our city. Dr. McMichael made the call to Houston. Miraculously, an appointment was scheduled for the following week.

We were introduced to Dr. Jankovic, a renowned professor of the neurology department of the Baylor College of Medicine. He proved to be one of the most intellectual and warm-hearted doctors that we had ever met. Dr. Jankovic spent four hours with us, asking questions about my medical history. He diagnosed me with Blepharospasm – *not* Tourette's Syndrome. He explained that Blepharospasm affects no age limit and has no direct cause. The Basal Ganglia in the brain sends messages that my eyelids need to close. Thus, spasms occur. He wanted to give the Botox injections in that very room, but I was terrified to receive them. When I explained my fears, he told me that the needles were too big from the other doctor. I braced myself for the excruciating pain, but really only felt a moderate burning and a sharp sting in the eyelids. He gave eight injections in each eyelid. He talked of everything to keep my mind off the pain from the shots.

On that first visit, he recommended that I get the *potosis crutches* for my glasses. At last, someone knew about these! We had only read about them on the Internet, but now we knew that they did indeed exist. Dr. Jankovic suggested that I use not only the drops for my eyes but a lubricating cream as well to keep my eyes from drying out during my sleep.

Before I go on, let me tell you about how God supplied my need for eye drops. While in New Zealand, I received a letter from a dear couple in our church, Alan and Sarah Van Zandt, saying that they wanted to supply me with eye drops for however long I needed them. Mark and I didn't even know this precious couple that had come into our lives. We were so humbled by their act of kindness and generosity. Alan presented my need to the eye drop company that he works for, and they agreed to supply me with eye drops, looking at my need as a mission project.

After receiving the painful shots, Mark led me downstairs to the ophthalmologist who invented this miraculous procedure known as the *ptosis crutch*. The special glasses were ordered, and I was fit for the crutches. It would take a couple of months to process the order. I was sure hoping to have them before we traveled to Brazil to renew our visas. Three days before our departure to Brazil, Dr. Jankovic gave me another round of injections. We prayed fervently that this time the shots would work.

Soon after my diagnosis, I started receiving a bi-monthly Bleparo-spasm newsletter through the efforts of two dear women. They paid for my subscription. When I received my first newsletter, I started crying, telling Mark that there were really people like me with this same disease. Story after story filled my heart with inspiration. There was a question and answer segment that I found very interesting. The Blepharospasm Foundation is located in Beaumont, Texas, founded by Mary Lou Koster. It touches so many hearts today. I'm so thankful for those two dear ladies who helped me to know others who face this disease with a fighting spirit.

It was so good to see our Brazilian friends again. I never realized how hard it would be to understand the Portuguese language without being able to see the people and their gestures. After a week in Brazil, I really began to question what the Lord wanted for my life. The shots had not performed as we had hoped, and I cried for about three days. Mark was such a source of encouragement, telling me that we would find the answers, just to rest in the Lord. At that time I was reminded of Psalms 37. I knew that if I *trusted* in the Lord, *delighted* in Him, and *committed* my life to Him, then I could finally *rest* in Him. That's exactly what I began to do – *Rest* in the Lord. How glorious those next few weeks were. I was able to joke about my disease. I was able to find humor in my situation.

From Brazil, we flew to Jerry Siler's church in Dayton, Ohio for their annual mission's conference. By the time we arrived, I was totally empty inside. I had nothing else to give. What I failed to realize was that God wanted to fill my cup with encouragement, strength, and most of all – His power. This realization came when Brother Siler brought a devotion to all the missionaries one morning. Tears started streaming down my face. I couldn't hold back the agony I was feeling inside. It felt so good to release it all. I guess you could say I was crying for myself. I had to be led around everywhere. Once again, my eyes were completely closed. I received strength from the other missionaries, Pastor Siler, members of his church, and most of all, from my devoted husband. The Lord has been so good to me to give me someone like Mark, who can share my pain, even though he may not understand what I'm going through.

By the end of the week, I felt like I was back to my old self again. Pastor Siler's conference was just the shot in the arm I needed to keep going. When we arrived in Nashville for Beacon Baptist's mission conference, I felt like I could conquer the world. Isn't it amazing how the Lord works? During the conference, the ladies of the church took the missionary wives shopping. I felt bad about the ladies having to lead me around, so I held one eye open as I walked. They couldn't bear for me to feel alone, so they did the same. You should have seen the looks we got. I wonder how many women in that mall are still wondering if that is the new fad. How hilarious we looked, but it felt so good to laugh. Remember what the Bible says about laughter, *Laughter is good for the soul.*

CHAPTER EIGHTEEN

THE PTOSIS CRUTCH

*I*continued to receive Botox injections every 3-to-4 months and took the prescribed 50-mg. of Amytriptilene, but the shots still didn't enable me to open my eyes. After the conference, we received word that my special glasses were ready to be picked up in Houston. I could barely contain myself! What would the glasses look like? Do you remember the TV character, Steve Urkell? Remember his round-rimmed coke bottle glasses? That's what I pictured myself.

Mark led me to a chair directly across from the ophthalmologist. I sat down, wondering how in the world this contraption would work. The ophthalmologist gently placed the glasses on my face and gingerly lifted my eyelids to rest on the wires. Yes, you read right. Wires were delicately attached to the inside of my glasses. I eventually learned the art of pulling my eyelids up and resting them on the wires that were attached to the inside of my glasses.

Oh, my glasses – I almost forgot. They were the prettiest shape, slightly larger than the standard frame, with a soft lilac design that shimmered in the light. I was pleasantly surprised. As my eyelids were lifted by the ophthalmologist, tears welled up in my eyes as I saw him smiling back at me. I began looking around at all the wonderful people who had a part in these extraordinary glasses. I jumped up and hugged everyone in the room. I think I even hugged all the other customers as well. It felt so good – for the first time in eight months

– to walk with my eyes staying open. Everything and everyone was so beautiful. For the first time in eight months, I was not *functionally blind*. We thanked everyone and headed for the car. On our way to the car, we passed person after person, suffering from their own battles of health. I wanted to shout to everyone that I was able to see! The ophthalmologist explained that my eyes would fight the wires for they were something new for my eyelids to. I still had spasms and my body did fight the wires on the glasses like the ophthalmologist said, but I didn't mind. It just felt so good to see!

From Houston, we drove to our next church in North Carolina. We stopped at a rest area to stretch. Remember the dreaded rest areas earlier in my story? Well, now I looked forward to them. As we were getting ready to leave the rest area, I convinced Mark to let me drive for a few minutes. He finally gave in to my request. It felt so good to be behind the wheel again. It felt good to be in control. Mark reluctantly reclined his seat to rest position for a few minutes. His few minutes of rest were short-lived, when I questioned him if the sign a few feet away was something that I needed to be aware of. He sat upright and quickly informed me that the right lane ahead was closed due to construction and instructed me to pull over. Apparently, my driving days were over. The following Sunday morning at Celebration Baptist Church in North Carolina, I was able to walk onto the platform without any help. I was bursting at the seams with joy. I know that Mark was rejoicing with me, but I think he secretly missed walking me to the front of the church.

Grocery shopping. Before receiving my glasses, Mark always did the grocery shopping. I would verbally give him a list; he would quickly write it down and then head down to the nearest grocery store. For him, it was a quick in and out trip. For me, grocery shopping for the first time using my ptosis crutch glasses was like a kid in a candy store.

Mark really did share in my enthusiasm, even though it meant taking extra time for me to compare prices, read the nutritional labels and find the coupons for particular products. It was so much fun and at the same time very overwhelming to see an entire aisle stocked with every kind of cereal imaginable. Deciding on laundry soap was just as time consuming. Mark said he used to just close his eyes and pick one. That way it took all the hassle out of choosing.

I recall having our pictures taken to distribute to our supporting churches and new churches that requested them. I was so pleased that my eyes were able to stay open with the ptosis crutch. The photographer positioned us for a family portrait, instructing us to focus on the blue dot. She was about ready to click the button when she paused and sweetly said to me, "Dear, could you open your eyes just a little bit more?" I suppressed a laugh, trying to maintain my composure. I thought about explaining my dilemma to her but realized that I would just confuse her more and add confusion to her hectic schedule. I was "wired up" for about a year-and-a-half. Technology is so amazing, isn't it? I praise the Lord for the doctors He has sent to me along the way. At the end of our furlough, I revisited Dr. Jankovic to discuss how long I would be able to safely use my glasses. Sitting in his office, he explained to me that the ptosis crutch is not a permanent remedy, just a temporary one; therefore, it should not be used any longer. He suggested that I see Dr. Patrinely, a renowned plastic surgeon that specializes in the eyelid and facial area.

From all that I have read of Dr. Patrinely, he is everything the books say he is. He is well informed of my condition with a very hospitable manner, like that of Dr. Jankovic. When Dr. Patrinely asked me take my glasses off and open my eyes, he noticed immediately where the real problem was. He explained that even though I have Blepharospasm, I also have what is known as *Apraxia of the Eyelid.*

This is where the patient tries his very hardest to open his eyes, but the eyelids lay dormant, refusing to open because of mixed signals from the brain. Soon after my visit with Dr. Patrinely, I received a video, through the mail, showing two types of surgeries that can be done for sufferers of Blepharospasm. A full myectomy and limited myectomy were two new words added to my vocabulary. These surgeries involve the cutting away of the squeezing muscles in the eyelids. After talking with Dr. Patrinely and sharing my fears with him about the two myectomy surgeries, he suggested that I have a surgery known as a *frontal sling* or *bi-lateral suspension*. Artificial tendons are placed in the forehead, connected to the eyebrows and finally to the eyelids. The surgery enables the patient to lift his eyebrows, which in turn lifts the eyelids to the point of being able to see. The Lord always takes care of our needs.

For I know that the Lord is great… (Psalm 119:105)

Thy word is a lamp unto my feet, and a light unto my path (Psalm 135:5a).

CHAPTER NINETEEN

A NEW LIFE

The day finally came for us to leave for Houston, Texas. We left a week early from Dallas to be in a mission conference in Corpus Cristi, and then planned to head for Houston on the following Sunday afternoon. My surgery was scheduled for eight o'clock Monday morning. Mark noticed a ticking noise halfway into our trip to Corpus. Suddenly, without any warning, our 1994 Ford Escort just stalled right in the middle of the freeway. We safely pulled to the side to inspect what had gone wrong. We knew it was more than just a loose hose. We were just outside of San Antonio. Whom would we call? Mark called a pastor friend in Saguine, Texas, who gave us the number of a pastor in Austin, Texas. That pastor gave us the name of a pastor in San Antonio.

Mark called the church and only received the answering machine. He left a voice mail on the machine, and not five minutes later, a young woman called us back to say that she was a member of the church and contacted her mother to come and pick me up to get me out of the heat. The church had a mechanic who came to our rescue. Our home church, Pleasantview Baptist, rented us a car until our own was repaired. We missed the conference that night but were able to make it for the Sunday morning services. Satan was out to destroy our plans of getting to Houston, but God is always faithful!

The following Monday morning, April 29, I was sitting in the office of Dr. Patrinely and nervous as all get out. My blood pressure was high, and I was running a low-grade fever. The nurses were unsure if I was just nervous or if I indeed had an infection. After being sedated, my vitals returned to normal. I remember waking shortly, realizing that for the first time in two years I was able to open my eyes. Dr. Patrinely was leaning over me to see how I was doing. I remember choking back my tears as I whispered, "I can see!" I thanked him a million times and called him my miracle doctor. For the next few weeks I looked like I had been in a boxing match.

After six weeks of recovery, I was overjoyed to regain some of my freedom, lost four years prior. Many other firsts were happening in my life all at once. Some examples are: grocery shopping without getting lost or running into someone else's cart. My first walk to the launderette with all my clothes intact in the basket; being able to cook with both eyes open instead of holding one eye open and stirring with the other hand; actually styling my own hair; (Now, that's definitely a priority) stopping at a rest area and not getting lost in the bathroom; not having the photographer ask, Ma'am, please open your eyes a little more;" picking out my own clothes and actually being presentable in public; not having to wonder whose shoes I am following; not having to drink coke through a straw or just being able to see while someone else was talking; most of all though, was being able to read God's precious Word.

Those are just a few of the gazillion firsts that I experienced during that period of my life. We were all anxious to move forward and be settled as a family again. The three-month period of waiting to make sure that my body accepted the suspension was nearing the end. Finally, on August 7, 2002, we boarded the plane headed for São Paulo, Brazil.

Even though I was thrilled to be back on the mission field, I was apprehensive at the same time. How would I explain my disease to people that have no clue about Blepharospasm? How would the people react to my spasms? Would I just scare off everybody? Would I be able to find a neurologist in São Paulo who was knowledgeable about Blepharospasm? My doctor in Houston recommended a neurologist in Belo Horizonte, a city about eight hours away by car. I called the doctor there and explained to him that I really wanted to stay in São Paulo if possible. He gave me a woman's name who dealt somewhat with Blepharospasm patients. After contacting her, she recommended Dr. Alexandre because of his experience with Botox injections.

I put the doctor's phone number in a safe place but then forgot where I put it. I no longer had the number of the woman who had given me the doctor's cell phone number. I was frantic. How would I find that doctor's number again?

I'm sure the Lord was just shaking his head saying, "Dana, Dana, Dana, don't you trust me to take care of you?"

While I was frantically searching for the number, Shaunna called one of her friends, but accidentally dialed the wrong cell phone number and heard a message on an answering machine. Because most cell phones have caller ID, the person to whom the cell phone belonged was able to call back. Guess whose wrong number Shaunna dialed? It was Dr. Alexandre. Isn't that incredible? The Lord is so amazing! I answered the phone, thrilled to learn that it was Dr. Alexandre. He spoke to me in English about my disease and scheduled an appointment for me to come in and have a round of Botox injections. When Dr. Alexandre learned that I was a patient of Dr. Jankovic's, his response was, "Oh, Dana, Dr. Jankovic is like the pope of neurology!" Dr. Alexandre commented to Mark and me that he had studied under Dr. Jankovic for six months in Houston, Texas.

Originally, our plans were to begin a new work in the city, but God impressed upon our hearts to stay in Vargem Grande, an area outside of the city, with a population of over 55,000 precious souls. Because the church had suffered greatly from some major setbacks, our goal was to re-build the Calvary Baptist Church – a work that we started back in 1994. The language seemed very strange to me. I knew that my cluttered brain had stored the Portuguese language somewhere. The question was where?

Stress is a known factor that causes any condition to worsen, so you guessed it: my spasms went haywire. As bewildered faces searched mine for answers, I knew that an explanation was in order. I sure didn't want them to think that I was some kind of a crazed woman waiting to cast a spell on them. They were all very patient and kind as I tried mercilessly to explain why my nose twitched, my mouth turned crooked at the corners, and why my eyes kept blinking. Since they could relate to the television series *Bewitched*, I told them that I was like her, except that I didn't go anywhere. That seemed to break the ice in a hurry. Everyone was laughing and joking. Thank you Lord!

I read an article entitled, *Advancing through Adversity,* which helped me to deal with the limited freedom I now experienced. No longer do I cross a street by myself. I heard a motto once from a missionary to Germany. He stated that there are two kinds of pedestrians: *a fast one and a dead one.* Well, since I'm certainly not a fast pedestrian, then I would surely be a dead one. Trust me, the green light at the cross-walk doesn't always mean that you can walk. I've always wondered why they made traffic lights in São Paulo.

Walking is very strenuous for me. If the path is rocky, then forget it. I'll just end up falling, taking someone down with me. That's not a pretty sight on visitation. Josefa, one of the faithful ladies in the church, asked me to make a visit with her. We decided that Sunday afternoon before church would be the best time for that particular visit. I was apprehensive, but I knew how much this meant to her. All prayed up, I ventured out onto the main dirt road keeping a light touch on her arm. Some people feel uncomfortable about leading a *blind* person, so I just casually stayed close to her side, hoping all the while that I could make it down to the end of the street.

As we approached the one-room house at the corner, I noticed gravel and sand flying around us. Some troublemakers or *moleques,* as they call them in Brazil, thought they would have some fun and nearly ran us down. My heart was beating so fast that I could barely breathe. Oh, to have Justin's BB gun with me! What a sight it would have been to see all their tires blown out. Okay, now you're probably wondering how a missionary's wife can have such evil thoughts. Well, don't worry, I repented, but it sure was fun imagining it.

The people had an afternoon service on Sundays and a mid-week service on Thursdays. Our prayer was that the Lord would give us strength and wisdom to lead the people to a spiritual maturity. By mid-afternoon on any given day, I was exhausted. I spent all my energy just working to keep my eyes functioning properly. I was totally dependent on the Lord to work through the ministry with the obstacles that lay ahead for me. Isn't that where the Lord wants us to be – totally dependent on Him?

About two months into the work, I talked to Mark about the idea of starting a Bible club on Thursday nights – the mid-week service. At the time, Linete and her two children, Ellen and Danillo, were the only people attending on Thursday nights. Mark was in favor of the club and knew that it would bring more prospects to the church. In three short months, we were running around twenty-five kids and teenagers. As a result of the Bible club, the kids started encouraging their parents to come out on Thursday nights. The life of the Brazilian in Vargem Grande is extremely hard and many times discouraging. As of 2005, sixty-five percent of the adults are unemployed. This percentage no doubt will continue to rise because of poverty that faces the outer lying edges of São Paulo. The bus system has improved remarkably, but for the rural areas, wake-up time is still a miserable 3:00 a.m. just to stand in line for an hour or so before being able to land a spot on the bus. You don't always have the luxury of sitting down for the two-hour bus ride into town. At least in the morning you don't have to contend with the body odor that results from being packed like sardines.

Justin knows this scenario all too well. At the young, tender age of seven, he was holding my hand as we sifted our way through the crowd on the dimly lit, overloaded bus. I lost his grip and frantically searched for him behind me. There he was, with a forlorn look about him, sandwiched like a sardine between two women's backsides. That memory is etched in my mind forever.

God will provide a way.

CHAPTER TWENTY

MAKING A DIFFERENCE

Justin is an adult now, serving in Iraq with the 101ˢᵗ Airborne Division. Since he was twelve years old, Justin has always commented that he wants to make a difference in life. He is definitely doing that – making a difference by serving his country, which he dearly loves. The Lord opened every door for him to enter the military. He graduated from basic training in April of 2003 in Fort Benning, Georgia. The ceremony was extraordinary with Justin looking so handsome in his dress uniform. We decided to celebrate this milestone in his life and chose a nice restaurant located off post.

We sat close to the restrooms – you know, just in case. Sure enough, my bladder was screaming. I calculated how many steps it would take to get to the restroom and made sure that no one was in my pathway. For some reason, as I exited the restroom, and rounded the corner, my spasms went haywire. My eyes started squinting, my nose twitched, and my mouth curved to one side. Coming my way was one of the waiters. As he passed, he looked my way, grinned and then winked at me. *Oh, no, did he think that I was flirting with him?* My mind was racing as I thought, *Should I explain my spasms to him? No, that would just cause more confusion.* I shared my story with Mark, Shaunna and Justin. Shaunna commented through her bursts of laughter, "Well, Mom, was he cute?"

During Justin's first tour of duty in South Korea, one of the soldiers in his unit invited him to the Shalom House, a Christian organization for men and women in the military, located off post. It was there that Justin met Bill Meyer, director of the Shalom House. He took Justin under his wing, discipling and mentoring him for the time that he was stationed in South Korea. Through Bill's teachings, Justin prepared his first Bible study to the group of soldiers in his unit. Even though none of the soldiers attended the Bible study, Justin still learned a great deal from what he had studied. Before leaving Korea, Justin was able to win one of the soldiers to a saving knowledge of Jesus Christ. Mark and I will forever be grateful for the discipleship that Justin received at the Shalom House.

The Lord did the same in Fort Campbell, Kentucky, sending Justin spiritual helps through the Navigators, a Christian-based organization that reaches out, not only to civilians, but military men and women as well.

When we returned to Brazil in 2002, the Lord gave us a beautiful home to rent, which was about a five-minute drive from the church. We bought two German shepherds and two cats, while Shaunna bought an adorable white rat, which she named Henry. As you can tell, we love animals. Shaunna's two parakeets serenaded us every morning with their beautiful songs. One beautiful summer day, I opened all the windows and doors to let the fresh air in.

As I cleaned, I noticed that Gabby, one of our German shepherds, was lying next to our bedroom door. I thought it strange, since that wasn't her favorite place to get comfortable. I didn't want to disturb her, for she was sleeping so comfortably. However, I became concerned when she didn't move from that spot for a long period of time. I decided that I'd better check on her. Xenia, our black German shepherd was following close behind. I was sure hoping that nothing was wrong with Gabby. I was surprised that Gabby didn't move as she heard me and Xenia walking down the hallway on the tiled floor. As I neared her, I was talking sweetly to her so I wouldn't startle her.

To my amazement, it wasn't Gabby at all – just a pile of dirty clothes! Surely, I was losing my mind!

The woman on the subway must have thought that very thing about me. Mark and I had taken the subway downtown to buy some Sunday school material. There was no room to sit, so I stood close to Mark with my hand just below his on the railing. I removed my hand to adjust my glasses, then grabbed the rail again. I was thinking to myself of how precious Mark is to me. With that thought in mind, I covered his hand with my hand, entwining my fingers with his. Guess what? It wasn't his hand! The woman quickly removed her hand and moved to another rail. I couldn't wait to get off that subway.

That story reminds me of the bus ride that the three of us were taking home one night from the mall. Shaunna has always been very protective of me – sometimes overprotective – especially when it came to riding the bus, train, or subway. I was fortunate to get a seat on the overcrowded bus. Mark and Shaunna were standing close by. Our stop was coming up, so I started gathering my belongings. As I stood up, I thought that I was re-living the story of the parting of the Red Sea. Suddenly, everyone in the aisle parted to the sides of the bus. I thought, *That was nice of them to do that, but it sure was strange.* Usually, you have to push your way through to get off of the bus in time.

I was thankful that all of us had gotten off the bus safely. I say that because sometimes the drivers take off without waiting to see if the passenger has both feet on the ground. On our way home, I said to Mark and Shaunna, "Did you see all those people move from the aisle to the side of the bus? It reminded me of the parting of the Red Sea." Shaunna matter-of-factly said, "Oh, yeah, I told them to watch out for you, mom, cause you're blind." I laughed and thought, *Well, at least I didn't have to fight my way through the crowd.*

CHAPTER TWENTY ONE

GOD'S WILL ACCOMPLISHED

*B*ecause God is the Great Physician, Shaunna has victoriously overcome the haunting fears stemming from her traumatic ordeal ten years ago, which had threatened to destroy her steadfast faith in our almighty God. Satan's primary goal was to take a sweet, generous, and loving Christian teenager and cause her to become a bitter vessel for Christ. Remember the A-Team's motto? *I love it when a plan comes together.* Well, I'm glad that Satan's plan to destroy Shaunna's faith *did not* come together. AMEN!

Shaunna worked alongside Mark and me for some time before returning to Arlington, Texas, to pursue her career. She brought new life to the church. Her teaching abilities are outstanding. She amazes everyone with her artistic talent that is displayed in the form of a mural on the classroom walls of two national's works. They love her carefree spirit and deep love for her Lord.

Justin continues his career as a Specialist with the 101st Airborne Division, stationed in Iraq. My prayer is that the Lord will keep him safe and use his strong leadership to lead others to Christ. My heart goes out to all the moms, dads, spouses and other family members who have lost their soldiers in the fight for freedom. We can't comprehend the immensity of God's grace but how wonderful it is to know that His grace can pull us through any tragedy.

I am a different person today because of the tragedy and adversity that has touched our family. I no longer take any given day for granted. Until the Lord cures me of my Blepharospasm, I will always be dependent on others. That used to bother me, but not anymore. I'm reminded of Habakkuk's words that we are to *rejoice* in the Lord, no matter what the circumstance may be. I am a stronger Christian today because of my Blepharospasm. Sure, I have my valleys that I walk through, but I know that I'm not alone.

Life has changed for both Mark and me. I'm sure that Mark never knew his job description would include being a fashion consultant, hair designer, or make-up artist. Mark is my inspiration. One of my treasured moments is when he reads the Bible to me. How precious God's Word is.

I'm on a new medication now – Effexor XR and Artane. Getting off of the Amytriptiline helped me to lose weight. Unfortunately, many medications cause weight gain. The Effexor and Artane are a great combination for me. I read recently that Effexor or other kinds of anti-depressants help women with their menopause symptoms. Oh, my menopause. I forgot to talk about those stories. Oh, well, guess I'll have to save those for another book.

On a final note, the church continues to grow in Vargem Grande. Many readers will remember the church robbery. The people were devastated, but they too knew that God had a plan. Through the robbery, the church was able to buy back everything lost. One of the prayers of the church people was that one day the building could be remodeled inside. The church building used to be a grocery store and still had the old tile on the walls. Well, the Lord provided the funds needed to remodel the inside of the church – through the robbery. Like our pastor, Dr. Moody, says, "Ain't God Good?"

When we return to Brazil, we'll be starting a new work in a completely different area of São Paulo. Some have asked if I'm nervous or scared. Well, I would be lying if I said no, but one thing I do know for sure: I'll definitely have more stories to tell. A new group of people will get used to my spasms, and we'll all laugh together while sitting around a dining room table eating bread, drinking coffee and talking about how marvelous God is and how He sustains us every day with His amazing grace. You see, the battle isn't mine, it's His. It's His grace that enables me to say, "Thank you, sweet Jesus. The Battle Has Been Won."

The grass withereth, the flower fadeth: but the word of our God shall stand for ever (Isaiah 40:8).

ABOUT THE AUTHOR

Hi. I'm Dana McCutchen, a missionary to São Paulo, Brazil. Are you going through a storm in your life? Have you been through one that seemed would never end? The reason I use the past tense is because God promises in His Word that He will never "leave us or forsake us." My story explains how God has allowed my family and me the ability to withstand trials and tragedy through His Grace and Mercy. I serve alongside my husband, Mark, the love of my life. I have two grown children, Shaunna and Justin. My prayer is that this book will encourage you to not give up when tragedy strikes. I serve a wonderful and mighty God who can deliver you from any life storm that comes your way.

Visit our ministry website

Like us on Facebook

Share this book on Facebook

Review this book on Amazon

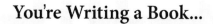